ASTROLOGY BOOKS IN PRINT

Para Research
Rockport, Massachusetts

International Standard Book Number: 0-914918-25-7

Typesetting by Paratext
Coordinated by Lucinda Pratt
Edited by Sarah Nevin and Marah Ren
Graphics by Marlene Comet

Printed by R.R. Donnelley & Sons Co.
on 55-pound cream white paper

Published by Para Research, Inc.
Whistlestop Mall
Rockport, Massachusetts 01966

Manufactured in the United States of America

First Printing May, 1981, 10,000 copies

How to Use This Book

Astrology Books in Print is directed toward all who are interested in published material on astrology. It has been published as a reference tool not only for the professional astrological counselor and researcher, the serious student and the individual who has turned or will turn to astrology seeking answers, but also for the librarian, the bookstore clerk, the researcher and that most valued of individuals, the bibliophile.

The staff at Para Research has sought to provide a complete listing of astrological books and magazines currently available in the general book marketplace. Availability is the key. *Astrology Books in Print* includes brief descriptions and complete bibliographic information on those books which the interested reader can obtain at a local bookstore or library. With the increasing interest and acceptance of astrology as a viable source of psychological and social insight, most bookstores and libraries throughout the United States have recognized the demand for astrological books that go beyond the popular daily forecast variety and have sought to provide well-stocked sections on astrology and metaphysics.

Not all of the titles listed in the following pages will be on the shelves of your nearest bookstore, of course; but with the information provided for each title, helpful bookstore staff will be able to obtain your selections through special orders to a publisher or wholesaler. Bookstores should stock those books frequently requested in order to meet the growing demand for quality astrological publications. You, as an astrologically interested customer, can assist your local bookstore in selecting the kind of material which appeals to you.

Information on the more than nine hundred entries in this book has been collected from publishers, wholesalers, astrological societies and professional astrologers throughout the United States and in some instances from foreign countries. References to material published outside the United States, however, have been kept to a minimum. Foreign books are cited only if they are in the English language and are readily available in this country. In these cases, a United States distributor with current stock of the book is cited in addition to the original publisher.

The body of astrological literature includes many self-published pamphlets and books. Most self-published material has limited circulation and can be so specialized in terms of subject and focus as to have limited appeal. Such material is not included in this volume. Again the key criteria concern availability. If a privately published volume has gained substantial popularity and is readily available, it has been included in *Astrology Books in Print* and can be ordered from the author or a distributor.

Much of the data provided for each title has been obtained directly from the publisher. The staff at Para Research has had to rely on publishers for reliable information on prices and current availability. Titles which may be on a few bookstore shelves at this moment but will be out of print in the near future have been excluded from *Astrology Books in Print*. Price and format information provided is current as of February 1981. Publishers retain the right to change prices, however, and Para Research is not responsible for price increases on the titles listed.

Descriptions of the books listed in this volume have been researched and written by the staff at Para Research. We have attempted to avoid the hyperbole of advertising copy and dustjacket blurbs, and to present brief, objective descriptions of the content and character of each book. We do not recommend any individual titles. The intent of this book is to let you know what publications are available. The choice as to the quality and appeal of particular books is yours alone. When possible, we suggest that you hold the book in your hand, look over the table of contents, read over parts of the book, particularly the introduction and conclusion. We lead you to the book; we do not attempt to make you read or buy it.

Astrology Books in Print is organized so that you can either browse through it looking for titles of interest or quickly and easily locate a specific title. We provide a special section of introductory material and comprehensive textbooks for the beginning astrologer. The bulk of the titles in *Astrology Books in Print* are listed alphabetically by title in the main section. A separate section is devoted to reference materials grouping ephemerides, data sourcebooks and dictionaries for your convenience. We have also provided several sections devoted to non-book materials: magazines, annuals and almanacs, calendars and chart blanks. An author index covering all sections is provided as well as an alphabetical index of the one hundred forty publishers cited by abbreviated code in the title listings.

Within each section, titles are listed alphabetically. Each listing in *Astrology Books in Print* begins with the title, followed by the author's name, price information, with p, c or s for paperback, clothbound or spiral bound edition, the number of pages (pp.) and the publisher's code. On books which the publisher has assigned an International Standard Book Number, the ISBN follows the price and edition information.

Any bookstore clerk or librarian can assist you in locating a title listed in *Astrology Books in Print.* If they cannot place the correct book in your hands immediately, they can order the book for you. If your local bookseller does not carry your requested title, remember that most large cities in the United States now include at least one bookstore specializing in astrological and metaphysical subject areas. These stores will be well-stocked in many of the titles listed in *Astrology Books in Print.* In general, the bookstore where you obtained this book has already indicated a desire to stock astrological reading material and is a good place to begin.

If after looking for your selected titles in local bookstores, you desire to order directly from the publisher, current addresses for all publishers cited in this book are provided in the alphabetical publisher index. It is wise to inquire whether the book can be ordered from the publisher before sending payment directly to the publisher. Only after determining that the publisher will ship the book directly to you and knowing additional handling and postage charges, if any, should you submit a prepaid order.

Astrology Books in Print has been published as a service to you, the reader interested in astrology. The staff at Para Research has tried to include listings of all current and projected publications available to you as of early 1981. With interest in astrology on the rise, books and magazines in this field are bound to proliferate. Current books will be revised, go out of print or be replaced by new titles. *Astrology Books in Print* is a good beginning place; it will be revised and expanded in future editions.

The usefulness and comprehensiveness of this first edition of *Astrology Books in Print* is primarily due to the steadfast attention to detail exercized by Lucinda Pratt, project coordinator, and to the editorial skills contributed by Sarah Nevin and Marah Ren. The staff at Para Research is proud of this contribution to astrological literature and hopes that it will be of use to bookpeople everywhere.

How well do you know yourself?

This horoscope gives you answers to these questions based on your exact time and place of birth...

How do others see you?
What is your greatest strength?
What are your life purposes?
What drives motivate you?
How do you think?
Are you a loving person?
How competitive are you?
What are your ideals?
How religious are you?
Can you take responsibility?
How creative are you?
How do you handle money?
How do you express yourself?
What career is best for you?
How will you be remembered?
Who are your real friends?
What are you hiding?

Many people are out of touch with their real selves. Some can't get ahead professionally because they are doing the wrong kind of work. Others lack self-confidence because they're trying to be someone they're not. Others are unsuccessful in love because they use the wrong approach with the wrong people. Astrology has helped hundreds of people with problems like these by showing them their real strengths, their real opportunities, their real selves.

You are a unique individual. Since the world began, there has never been anyone exactly like you. Sun-sign astrology, the kind you see in newspapers and magazines, is all right as far as it goes. But it treats you as if you were just the same as millions of others who have the same Sun sign because their birthdays are close to yours. A true astrological reading of

your character and personality has to be one of a kind, unlike any other. It has to be based on exact date, time, longitude and latitude of your birth. Only a big IBM computer like the one that Para Research uses can handle the trillions of possibilities.

A Unique Document Your Astral Portrait includes your complete chart with planetary positions and house cusps calculated to the nearest minute of arc, all planetary aspects with orbs and intensities, plus text explaining the meaning of:

★ Your particular combination of Sun and Moon signs.
★ Your Ascendant sign and the house position of its ruling planet. (Many computer horoscopes omit this because it requires exact birth data.)
★ The planets influencing all twelve houses in your chart.
★ Your planetary aspects.

Others Tell Us "I found the Astral Portrait to be the best horoscope I've ever read."—E.D., Los Angeles, CA
"I could not put it down until I'd read every word...It is like you've been looking over my should since I arrived in this world!"—B.N.L., Redding, CA
"I recommend the Astral Portrait. It even surpasses many of the readings done by professional astrologers."
—J.B., Bristol, CT

Low Price There is no substitute for a personal conference with an astrologer, but a good astrologer charges $50 and up for a complete chart reading. Some who have rich clients get $200 and more. Your Astral Portrait is an analysis of your character written by some of the world's foremost astrologers, and you can have it not for $200 or $50 but for only $20. This is possible because the text of your Astral Portrait is already written. You pay only for the cost of putting your birth information into the computer, compiling one copy, checking it and sending it to you within two weeks.

Permanance Ordinarily, you leave an astrologer's office with only a memory. Your Astral Portrait is a thirty-five page, fifteen-thousand-word, permanently bound book that you can read again and again for years.

Money-Back Guarantee Our guarantee is unconditional. That means you can return your Astral Portrait at any time for any reason and get a full refund. That means we take all the risk, not you!

You Hold the Key The secrets of your inner character and personality,

your real self, are locked in the memory of the computer. You alone hold the key: your time and place of birth. Fill in the coupon below and send it to the address shown with $20. Don't put it off. Do it now while you're thinking of it. Your Astral Portrait is waiting for you.

© 1977 Para Research, Inc.

1

Introductory Textbooks

ABC BASIC CHART READING, Lynne Palmer. $5.75p 52pp. AFA74. This guide to horoscope interpretation views the houses, aspects and planets as either harmonious or discordant. The material is condensed into keywords and phrases, a system which the author feels captures the essence of chart patterns.

ABC OF CHART ERECTION, Lynne Palmer. $8.50p 212pp. AFA71. Not intended for the beginning student, this manual is useful as a reference work for reviewing both elementary and advanced techniques. It includes many examples, tables and graphic illustrations.

A MANUAL OF ASTROLOGY or THE BOOK OF THE STARS, Raphael. $6.00s facsimile reprint (1837) 356pp. HEA. The author presents the art of foretelling future events by the influence of the heavenly bodies.

ASTROLOGER'S HANDBOOK, Frances Sakoian and Louis Acker. $12.95c ISBN 0-06-013734-7, 460pp. HAR73. Delineations of planetary aspects constitute the main portion of this comprehensive, introductory text. Instructions for casting and interpreting a natal horoscope are given as well as directions for ordering a personalized and computerized natal chart, with a tabulation of the native's planetary aspects, cross referenced to the proper pages of the book.

ASTROLOGER'S MANUAL, Landis Green. $6.95p ISBN 0-668-04200-1; $11.95c ISBN 0-668-03616-8, 255pp. ARC75. Green reviews the history of astrology and gives a detailed analysis of the elements, houses, twelve signs, house patterns of planetary distribution, Sun, Moon, astrological categories and human relationships.

ASTROLOGY: An Illustrated Manual for Teachers and Students, Pat Benis Miller. $6.00s 62pp. MAC. Organized as a general introduction, the book's twelve lessons cover the symbolism of the zodiac and planets, planetary rulerships and delineations, the houses, aspects, casting the chart, Moon's nodes, Part of Fortune, critical degrees, parallels, finding, indexing and marking aspects, progressions, transits, lunations and eclipses, and solar returns.

ASTROLOGY FOR ALL, Alan Leo. $6.95p ISBN 0-89281-175-7, 348pp. INT/WEI69. Leo's concise, easy-to-understand introduction to astrology includes background material, an analysis of the characteristics of each of the signs, a description of the Sun and Moon through the signs and the significance of the planets in each of the signs. Complete delineations of the twelve zodiacal types and the one hundred forty-four sub-types born each year are provided.

ASTROLOGY FOR THE MILLIONS, Grant Lewi. $2.95p 358pp. BAN69; $10.00c ISBN 0-87542-441-4, 257pp. LLE79. Lewi teaches the basics of casting a horoscope and projecting that horoscope into the future to predict upcoming events. Included are tables for determining solar, lunar and planetary positions from 1870 through 1999, projection tables, interpretations of natal positions and the influence of transiting planets. This book applies astrology to daily living.

ASTROLOGY: HOW AND WHY IT WORKS, Marc Edmund Jones. $2.95p ISBN 0-394-73442-4, 364pp. SHA45; $13.50c ISBN 0-87878-005-X, 448pp. AFA. This comprehensive explanation of astrological symbolism and the elements of astrological prediction includes discussions of the planets, signs and houses. The author identifies the origin of astrology as primitive man's confrontation with a world of chance and risk. Astrology effectively locates the individual in the orderliness of the universe. This is not recommended as a beginning text.

ASTROLOGY IN ONE DAY, Magnus Jensen. $2.50s facsimile reprint 35pp. HEA. Franklin D. Roosevelt's nativity is used to illustrate how to cast and read a horoscope.

ASTROLOGY MADE EASY, Astarte. $3.50p ISBN 0-87980-009-7, 192pp. WIL67. This book is a practical introduction to the science and art of astrology. It explains how the astronomical positions of the Sun, Moon, planets and stars at the exact moment of birth can be used to interpret and predict personal character and fate.

ASTROLOGY MADE EASY, H.F. $2.50, facsimile reprint 54pp. HEA. The influence of the stars and planets upon human life.

ASTROLOGY MADE PRACTICAL, Alexandra Kayhle. $3.00p ISBN 0-87980-010-0, 160pp. WIL67. This book shows how to interpret personality and behavior from astrology, number and body type, to enhance self-understanding and bring about self-realization.

ASTROLOGY WORKBOOK, Louise Ward. $15.00p 100pp. THS69. Designed to be used as a textbook and reference work, the five sections in this beginner's workbook define the signs and planets and teach horoscope erection. Worksheets are provided to help the student do secondary progressions, calculate house cusps, planetary positions, aspects and midpoints.

NEW A TO Z HOROSCOPE MAKER AND DELINEATOR, Llewellyn George. $17.95c ISBN 0-87542-263-2, 600pp. LLE80. Revised and edited by Marylee

Bytheriver. For more than seventy years this book has been used as an introductory textbook, dictionary and reference book by professionals, teachers, practicing and beginning students. It covers a wide range of astrological techniques from casting a natal or progressed chart, theories, lunations, use of the ephemeris and much more. This work is fully indexed and illustrated.

BASIC ASTROLOGY: A Guide for Teachers and Students, Joan Negus. $4.95p 124pp. AST79. This basic astrology text offers a systematic, introductory method for beginners as well as a good manual for teachers. The author emphasizes the principles of astrology more than the complex details of chart interpretation. Accompanying workbook available.

BASIC ASTROLOGY: A Workbook for Students, Joan Negus. $2.95p 60pp. AST79. Includes charts and tables needed for the carefully conceived program of homework assignments suggested at the end of each chapter in BASIC ASTROLOGY: A Guide for Teachers and Students.

BASIC ELEMENTS OF ASTROLOGY, Dorothy Hughes. $3.00p 37pp. AFA70. A basic overview of the wide scope of material available today on astrology.

BASIC PRINCIPLES OF ASTROLOGY, American Federation of Astrologers. $1.00p 64pp. AFA62. An AFA evaluation of the past, present and future nature of astrology.

BASICS OF ASTROLOGY, Ove H. Sehested. $14.95c URA73. Volumes I, II and III of Basics of Astrology are combined in one volume.

BASICS OF ASTROLOGY Vol I, Ove H. Sehested. $4.95 URA73. Chart erection is explained in detail.

BASICS OF ASTROLOGY Vol II, Ove H. Sehested. $4.95 URA73. The author presents a new and original technique for chart interpretation.

BASICS OF ASTROLOGY Vol III, Ove H. Sehested. $3.95 URA73. Tables and reference material are included for erecting and delineating a natal chart.

CHART YOUR OWN HOROSCOPE: For Beginner and Professional, Ursula Lewis. $2.50p 192pp. PIN76. A general handbook covering most of the basic aspects of astrology. The author discusses chart erection and interpretation, chart comparison techniques, aspects and transits. Tables are included.

COMPLEAT ASTROLOGER, Julia Parker and Derek. $9.95p BAN71. An illustrated work that presents the history of astrology, interpretations, progressions and the astronomical basics of astrology. Tables and an ephemeris from 1900 to 1975 are included.

ESSENTIALS OF ASTROLOGICAL ANALYSIS, Marc Edmund Jones. $16.50c ISBN 0-87878-011-4, 455pp. AFA60. This exposition of horoscope interpretation views human personality, as shown in each horoscope's unique pattern of potentials. Jones explains how to sift through astrological factors and order their relative importance effectively, avoiding confusion and irrelevant generalities and facilitating incisive analysis and dependable astrological counsel.

ESSENTIALS OF NATAL INTERPRETATION, Thyrza Escobar. $10.00p AFA.

EVERYBODY'S ASTROLOGY, Magnus Jensen. $2.50p facsimile reprint (1922) 48pp. HEA. This time-zone map covers the first twenty-five years after the adoption of Standard Time.

EVERYTHING YOU WANT TO KNOW ABOUT ASTROLOGY, NUMEROLOGY, HOW TO WIN, Zolar. $1.50p ISBN 0-668-02656-1, ARC.

GUIDE TO ASTROLOGY, Raphael. $5.00s facsimile reprint (1898) 200pp. HEA. Complete system of directions in genethliacal astrology.

HEAVEN KNOWS WHAT, Grant Lewi. $2.95p 497pp. BAN75; $10.00c ISBN 0-87542-442-2, 364pp. LLE62. This popular beginner's manual explains Grant Lewi's method of chart erection which does not require the complicated math usually needed. There are easy step-by-step instructions for casting charts. Tables covering 1890-1999 give the positions of the Sun, Moon and planets to be placed on the horoscope wheels which are included.

HIGHSCHOOL ASTROLOGY, Maud Reinertsen. $5.95c 130pp. UNI78. This textbook is an introduction to the basic principles of metaphysics and the fundamentals of astrological science.

HOW TO INTERPRET A BIRTH CHART, Martin Freeman. $7.00p ISBN 0-85030-249-8, 128pp. AQU81. The basic techniques of natal chart interpretations including how to interpret the planets, signs, houses, aspects and nodes, are explained.

INSTANT ASTROLOGY, Mary Orser and Rick and Glory Brightfield. $5.95p ISBN 0-06-090482-8, 146pp. HAR76. A positive approach is taken in this organized presentation of basic astrology, including instant astrology charts and wheels.

IN THE BEGINNING, ASTROLOGY, Ivy M. Goldstein-Jacobson. $11.00c 237pp. GOJ75. This book covers many diverse areas, including how to do prenatal astrology without mathematics, rectification of birthtime, vocational and mundane astrology and an expansion of the delineation material she presented in Simplified Horary Astrology. Technical instructions and numerous example charts are provided.

INTRODUCTION TO ASTROLOGY, William Lilly. $4.95p ISBN 0-87877-014-3; $10.95c ISBN 0-87877-314-2, 346pp. NCP72. This classic astrological manual will orient the new student and its older style will interest the more advanced student.

IT'S ALL IN THE STARS, Zolar. $2.95p ISBN 0-668-02542-5, 318pp. ARC62. Sun-sign compatibility is used to evaluate potential marriage partners. Interpretations of each degree of each sign and an explanation of the planets and houses are given.

LAYMAN'S HANDBOOK ON NUMEROLOGY AND ASTROLOGY, Edward M. Hughes. $7.00c 221pp. EHU76. Hughes' book contains the basics of numerology, Far-East astrology, Moon ephemeris, ascendant charts, a glossary and astro-poetry.

LET'S LEARN ASTROLOGY, Patricia Crossley. $7.50c ISBN 0-682-47727-3, 96pp. EXP72. This beginner's workbook teaches horoscope preparation, basic astrological principles and how to read and use an ephemeris and table of houses. The author discusses aspects, lunations and eclipses, rulerships and exaltations, the solar chart, elements and qualities, planetary disposition and parallels of declinations. Charts, diagrams and tables illustrate the book.

LOOKING AT ASTROLOGY, Liz Greene. $4.95p ISBN 0-916360-13-X CRC80. This full-color book for children has a section for every Sun sign.

MANUAL OF ASTROLOGY, Sepharial. $15.40p ISBN 0-572-01029-X, WFO. This is a standard work in four books: Treating of the Language of the Heavens, The Reading of a Horoscope, The Measure of Time and Hindu Astrology.

MODERN TEXT BOOK OF ASTROLOGY, Margaret E. Hone. $15.00c ISBN 85243-357-3, 315pp. FOW51. Margaret Hone, the founder of the Faculty of Astrological Studies of Great Britain, focuses this general text on establishing a sound basis of knowledge upon which further experience can be built. It is suitable for beginners' self-study and as a handbook for experienced astrologers.

MORNINGLAND ASTROLOGY BOOK ONE, Sri Patricia. $7.95s ISBN 0-935146-05-9, 262pp. MOR. The author maintains that this revolutionary approach to astrology, a telepathic journey through the Sun Dome, increases intelligence and promises a fascinating journey through the mind.

MORNINGLAND ASTROLOGY BOOK TWO, Sri Patricia. $7.95p ISBN 0-935146-06-7, 256pp. MOR. In her second work in this trilogy, the author presents her theory of how to walk the Path to Christ Consciousness through astrology; how to work with strategic command forces and available pyramids of power to assist in personal growth and evolution.

MORNINGLAND ASTROLOGY BOOK THREE, Sri Patricia. $7.95s ISBN 0-935146-07-5, MOR. In this third book in the series, the author discusses the wheel of Samsara or reincarnation and the view that the individual must complete a spiritual mission to reach enlightenment and leave the Earthly dimension.

MORNINGLAND ASTROLOGY CHART CONSTRUCTION, $3.50s ISBN 0-935146-10-5 MOR. This manual is designed to make chart construction easy and fun, proving that it is not necessary to be a mathematical wizard to calculate an astrological chart. Illustrations, diagrams and plenty of practice exercises are included.

NEW INSTANT ASTROLOGER, James A. Eshelman and Tom Stanton. $8.95c 184pp. APR/ASA. This fundamental beginner's text presents the essential principles of sidereal astrology. It contains the only detailed analyses of sidereal sign meanings in print. Chart comparison (synastry) and basic forecasting methods included, plus many useful tables.

THE ONLY WAY TO LEARN ASTROLOGY Vol 1, Marion March and Joan McEvers. $9.95p ISBN 0-917086-00-7, 246pp. AST76. The basics of astrology are presented and discussed in this textbook. It is organized as a series of self-explanatory lessons with test questions and answers at the end of each chapter.

THE ONLY WAY TO LEARN ASTROLOGY Vol 2, Marion March and Joan McEvers. 9.95p ISBN 0-917086-26-0, 320pp. AST81. A continuation of the authors' first volume, this book contains simple, direct instructions for all mathematical calculations, explains all the hows and whys, anticipates questions and provides answers.

PIE IN THE SKY: A Child's Book on Astrology, Lou McCulloch. $2.50p; $7.95c VUL80. This delightful story introducing astrology is aimed at the primary grades.

PRACTICE OF ASTROLOGY, Dane Rudhyar. $2.50p ISBN 0-394-73576-5, 152pp. SHA68. Astrology is seen here as a means to increase human knowledge and to satisfy man's yearning for harmony, by being attuned to celestial patterns and the basic order that exists in the universe.

PRINCIPLES AND PRACTICE OF ASTROLOGY, Vol 1: Horoscope Construction, Noel Tyl. $3.95p ISBN 0-87542-800-2, 239pp. LLE74. This totally self-contained volume explains the construction of a horoscope with the use of tables and practice horoscope blanks. It gives information on measuring the houses, astrological symbols, measuring planetary movement, the elements, polarities, nodes and the ruling planets. Test horoscopes are provided.

PRINCIPLES AND PRACTICE OF ASTROLOGY, Vol II: The Houses: Their Signs and Planets, Noel Tyl. $3.95p ISBN 0-87542-801-0, 142pp. LLE74. Tyl presents the rationale of house demarcation, the meanings of the signs upon each house, the planets' significance in every house and gives derivative house readings.

PRINCIPLES AND PRACTICE OF ASTROLOGY, Vol III: The Planets: Their Signs and Aspects, Noel Tyl. $3.95p ISBN 0-87542-802-0, 175pp. LLE74. A reference book for horoscope interpretation that gives a full explanation of the elements and nodes in a refreshing, modern style. Tyl articulates the significance of every planet within every sign, provides the reading of aspects and dignities and suggests meanings for all major aspects and Sun-Moon combinations.

PRINCIPLES AND PRACTICE OF ASTROLOGY, Vol IV: Aspects and Houses in Analysis, Noel Tyl. $3.95p ISBN 0-87542-803-7, 149pp. LLE74. This analytical synthesis of astrological techniques is presented through many examples, showing hemisphere emphasis, retrogradation patterns, the grand trine, the grand square, the T-square in complete explanation, the lunar nodal axis, parallels of declination, and the Part of Fortune. This volume is devoted totally to the art of synthesis.

PRINCIPLES AND PRACTICE OF ASTROLOGY, Vol V: Astrology and Personality, Noel Tyl. $3.95p ISBN 0-87542-804-5, 166pp. LLE74. Tyl explains psychological theories of personality translated into astrological terms and technique. He works with the theories of Kurt Lewin, Carl Jung, Henry Murray, Abraham Maslow, Erich Fromm, Alfred Adler and Sigmund Freud. An astrological glossary of psychological terms and personality traits is also included.

PRINCIPLES AND PRACTICE OF ASTROLOGY, Vol VI: The Expanded Present, Noel Tyl. $3.95p ISBN 0-87542-805-3, 189pp. LLE74. This is an introduction to prediction and an analysis of the time dimension in astrology. Topics include application and separation of aspects, "rapport" measurements, secondary progression, primary directions,"factor 7" analysis. Many examples clarify the work of astrology toward understanding change and development in personality, within free-will and fate.

PRINCIPLES AND PRACTICE OF ASTROLOGY, Vol VII: Integrated Transits, Noel Tyl. $3.95p ISBN 0-87542-806-1, 244pp. LLE74. A definitive work, modernizing the rationale, analysis and application of transit theory, in accord with the needs and expectations of modern people. Astrology is translated into behavior with many real-life examples for every major transit. The work also includes studies of solar revolution, rectification, eclipse theory, and accidents.

PRINCIPLES AND PRACTICE OF ASTROLOGY, Vol VIII: Analysis and Prediction, Noel Tyl. $3.95p ISBN 0-87542-807-X, 171pp. LLE74. A gallery of astrological portraits illustrates the whole view of astrological analysis, inspection of the past, expansion of the present and the creation of the future. Each step of deduction, analysis and projection is presented. Radix methods, progressions, and transits are fully interpreted. An introduction to Horary and Electional Astrology is included.

PRINCIPLES AND PRACTICE OF ASTROLOGY, Vol IX: Special Horoscope Dimensions, Noel Tyl. $3.95p ISBN 0-87542-808-8, 206pp. LLE75. A variety of topics are reviewed in this volume including chart comparisons, sex, love, abortion, homosexuality, vocation, relocation, opportunity and elections, illness, surgery and physical vitality.

PRINCIPLES AND PRACTICE OF ASTROLOGY, Vol X: Astrological Counsel, Noel Tyl. $3.95p ISBN 0-87542-809-6, 161pp. LLE75. Tyl's detailed inspection of the psychodynamics of the astrologer-client relationship with examples shows the astrologer's consideration of the horoscope and the individual. Difficulties are analyzed and communication techniques are explored.

PRINCIPLES AND PRACTICE OF ASTROLOGY, Vol XI: Astrology: Astral, Mundane, Occult, Noel Tyl. $3.95p ISBN 0-87542-810-X, 176pp. LLE75. A voyage through the astrology of nations to the fixed stars and beyond introduces mundane astrology governing international events. A discussion of Israel, Arabia, Germany, and the United States follows. Tyl also covers solar ingresses, great conjunctions, sign subdivision, degree symbolism, karma and reincarnation.

PRINCIPLES AND PRACTICE OF ASTROLOGY, Vol XII: Times to Come, Noel Tyl. $3.95p ISBN 0-87542-811-8, 197pp. LLE75. An introduction to the techniques of cosmobiology, sidereal astrology and the Uranian system gives the philosophical and behavioral parallels involving the art of creative compromise, remembrance of things past, and creative visualization.

PRINCIPLES OF ASTROLOGY, Charles E.O. Carter. $3.75p ISBN 0-8356-0423-3; $10.95c ISBN 0-8356-5138-X, 188pp. THE83. This revised edition of Carter's introductory textbook provides basic and essential astrological facts and explains how these facts affect human life.

STEP INTO ASTROLOGY I: The Fundamentals of Astrology, Angela Louise Gallo. $8.50p 134pp. CHM69. This basic textbook for the beginning student explains the fundamentals for the houses, signs and planets. Instructions are also given for reading an ephemeris.

STEP INTO ASTROLOGY II: Complete Mathematics Simplified - The Gallo Method, Angela Louise Gallo. $7.50p 58pp. CHM69. The author shows the beginning student how to calculate a natal and progressed chart with simplified mathematics.

STEP INTO ASTROLOGY III: Advanced Delineation, Angela Louise Gallo. $7.50p 100pp. CHM71. Instuctions are given for knowing where to start reading the chart, grouping houses, horary astrology and progressed charts.

STORY OF ASTROLOGY, Manly Palmer Hall. $6.75c ISBN 0-89314-525-4, 156pp. PHR75. Hall traces the history of astrology from ancient times to the present and includes its development in both the Far East and Western continents. The effect of astrology on the development of science, religion and philosophy is examined with special emphasis placed upon the astrological theories of the Greeks, Romans, Arabs and Aztecs.

SUN-SIGN PERSONALITY GUIDE, Robin MacNaughton. $2.95p ISBN 0-553-12805-1, 506pp. BAN78. Detailed. The twelve signs and one hundred forty-four combinations are listed for compatibility, money, sex, love, career, marriage, friends, health and more.

TEACHING AND STUDY GUIDE TO THE PRINCIPLES AND PRACTICE OF OF ASTROLOGY, Noel Tyl. $17.95c ISBN 1-87542-812-6, 650pp. LLE76. The overall goal of the twelve volume series is to systematically teach all aspects of astrology. The lessons accentuate the finer points of analysis, synthesis and application. Intended for both teachers and students, the book supplies many charts, illustrations, marginal subtopic notations and expounded discussions of topics discussed throughout the series.

TEXT-BOOK OF ASTROLOGY, A.J. Pearce. $10.00c 468pp. AFA70. This recent reprint covers both basic and complex astrological concepts and techniques as well as stressing the spiritual aspects of astrology. Pearce develops a good analysis of Ptolemy's techniques.

YOUR CHARACTER FROM THE STARS, Cole. $2.25p WEI. Sun signs and the physical characteristics of the signs and planets are explored here.

2

General Astrology

ABC OF MAJOR PROGRESSIONS, Lynne Palmer. $8.50p 162pp. AFA70. This technically-detailed volume outlines various methods for doing progressions. Recommended for the advanced astrologer, it includes many tables and practical examples.

ACD/LD METHOD OF PROGRESSIONS SIMPLIFIED, Sandra McDow and Jo Anna Graziano. $1.50p 12pp. AFA76. The ACD/LD method is clearly demonstrated with the aid of examples.

ADVANCED MATH FOR ASTROLOGICAL STUDENTS, J. Allen Jones. $10.00p ISBN 0-912368-15-2, GOL78. This includes once around the wheel directions (mundane) plus six thousand years of Jupiter-Saturn conjunctions.

A GUIDE TO QABALISTIC ASTROLOGY, Horus. $2.50p WEI. Aleister Crowley's version of Qabalah is a prerequisite for understanding this work. For serious students, the author outlines the Qabalistic system of astrological rulerships, octaves and exaltations. He presents a reconstitution of the astrological tree of life and discusses Pluto in Crowley's chart.

ALAN OKEN'S COMPLETE ASTROLOGY, Alan Oken. $9.95p ISBN 0-553-1262-2, 688pp. BAN80. This volume includes Oken's previously published works: AS ABOVE-SO BELOW, THE HOROSCOPE: THE ROAD AND ITS TRAVELERS, and ASTROLOGY: EVOLUTION AND REVOLUTION. Chart construction techniques are described and basic astrological concepts are explained.

A LIVING PERSON, Marc Robertson. $3.50p AFA. The author illustrates how human functions are symbols of all the signs, houses and planets.

ALL OVER THE EARTH ASTROLOGICALLY, Ivy M. Goldstein-Jacobson. $7.50c 215pp. GOJ63. This book focuses on the natal and progressed chart with a section on transits. It includes a good dictionary of astrology terminology and sixteen chart illustrations. The author presents astrology as a vehicle for inner growth and self understanding.

AMERICA: AN ASTROLOGICAL PORTRAIT OF ITS CITIES AND STATES: With a Special Section on Canada, Marc Penfield. $14.95s ISBN 0-914350-14-5, 448pp. VUL76. This well-researched complete reference work provides birthtimes and natal charts for all the states, provinces and major cities of the U.S. and Canada, with supplemental historical information for each location. A progressed U.S. horoscope is cast for St. Augustine, Florida, the first permanent settlement in this country.

AMERICAN BOOK OF CHARTS, Lois M. Rodden. $15.95p ISBN 0-917086-23-6, 411pp. AST80. Rodden presents five hundred accurate and verifiable birthcharts, citing sources for her data. Any data which the author could not verify is contained in an additional seven hundred biographical sketches. The significance of THE AMERICAN BOOK OF CHARTS is that Lois Rodden provides verification of previously suspect birth data and introduces a system of ranking verifiable data, which will become standard procedure among practicing astrologers.

AMERICAN BOOK OF MEDICAL ASTROLOGY, Eileen Nauman. $14.95p ISBN 0-917086-28-7, 368pp. AST81. This comprehensive reference book covers the latest astrological techniques of medicine and diagnosis, including extensive discussion of holistic nutrition and applications. Modern medical astrology teams up with science to prove its usefulness in diagnosis and recovery from disease.

AN ASTROLOGICAL GUIDE TO SELF-AWARENESS, Donna Cunningham. $5.95p ISBN 0-916360-09-01, 200pp. CRC78. Explores the deeper meanings of the planets, houses, aspects and transits, emphasizing self-understanding, personal growth and the importance of accepting self-responsibility. Written from a psychological perspective, this book provides specific tools for applying astrology to one's own life.

AN ASTROLOGICAL MANDALA, Dane Rudhyar. $3.95p 392pp. RAN73. Rudhyar revises interpretations of the Sabian symbols, those symbolic images for each of the 360 degrees in the zodiac. His work is designed to be used as a contemporary American I-Ching. He sees the Sabian symbols as three hundred sixty symbolic phases of the cycle of transformation.

AN ASTROLOGICAL STUDY OF PSYCHOLOGICAL COMPLEXES, Dane Rudhyar. $4.50p ISBN 0-394-73174-3, SHA. Rudhyar integrates significant features of astrology with Jungian psychology to show how the causes of emotional, social and sexual complexes can be better understood.

ANCIENT ASTROLOGY, THEORY AND PRACTICE, trans. Jean Rhys Bram. $15.00c ISBN 0-8155-5037-5, 336pp. NOY75. Here is the first English translation from the Latin of the Matheseos Libri VIII of Firmicus Maternus, written in the 4th century AD. This was the last treatise on astrology in the classical western world written before penalties were exacted against non-Christian practices. It also constitutes an extraordinary historical document, since Firmicus drew on Hellenistic, Egyptian and Syrian as well as Roman sources.

ANCIENT MASONRY, C.C. Zain. $9.00p ISBN 0-87887-347-3, 416pp. CHU73. The three-fold interpretation of every ritual and symbol of ancient masonry is fully explained. The astrological meaning and derivation for every symbol, as applied to the individual and to mankind as a whole, are given.

APPLIED ASTROLOGY, Margaret E. Hone. $7.25p ISBN 85243-073-6, 119pp. FOW53. This textbook is the companion volume to THE MODERN TEXT BOOK OF ASTROLOGY. It includes case histories which illustrate astroanalysis, examples of chart interpretation with marginal astrological references, and many diagrams.

APPLIED COSMOBIOLOGY, Reinhold Ebertin. $13.50p 208pp. HBV72. A basic but technical book explaining the use of the ninety degree dial, its evolution and application. Ebertin's exposition on the application of cosmological concepts for day to day living contains many easily understood illustrations.

APPROACHING AND DEPARTING ASPECTS, Frances Sakoian and Louis Acker. $2.75p 38pp. NES74. This in-depth study of aspects first looks at the general meaning of each aspect and then explores the approaching, departing, applying and separating phase of each aspect. The authors analyze the conjunction, opposition, square, trine, sextile, semisextile, semisquare, quintile, decile, tridecile, sesquiquadrate, biquintile, quincunx and vigintile.

APPROXIMATE POSITIONS OF ASTEROIDS 1900-1999, Emma Donath. $2.50p 23pp. EDO/AFA76.

APRIL 4, 1981 PIVOTAL DAY IN A CRITICAL YEAR, Jim Gross. $7.00p ISBN 0-933646-12-7, 168pp. ARI. Six innovative authors individually describe probable events surrounding this date involving mundane, personal interpretations and babies born on this day. Contributing articles are by Jim Lewis, Moby Dick, John Sandbach, Rusty Smith Carnarius and Philip Sedgwick.

ARCANA OF ASTROLOGY, W.J. Simmonite. $4.95p ISBN 0-87877-026-7; $10.95c ISBN 0-87877-326-6, 434pp. NPC74. This recent reprint is for the experienced astrologer. Related questions and answers follow each chapter. Mathematical and astronomical tables are included.

ART OF ASTROLOGY, Sheila Geddes. $15.95c ISBN 0-85030-250-1, 208pp. WEI81. The first edition in this complete course explains the working techniques of natal astrology. It is fully illustrated and enables anyone to set up a birth chart with professional accuracy.

ART OF ASTROLOGY, Sheila Geddes. $25.00c ISBN 0-85030-207-2, 208pp. AQU80. This complete course in the working techniques of natal astrology is specially written to comply with the syllabuses of most teaching institutions for career-minded students. It also provides guidance to the new astrologer for setting up and interpreting natal charts with professional accuracy.

ART OF CHART SYNTHESIS, Tracy Marks. $5.00p ISBN 0-933620-03-9, 112pp. SAG79. A step-by-step method is provided for interpreting the chart as a whole and determining its primary characteristics. Practice exercises in synthesis and interpretation are included.

ART OF FORECASTING, Sophia Mason. $4.00p 60pp. MAS. The author discusses predictive techniques, general forecasting and a simple way to"proofread" events indicated by the new, full and quarter Moons. "Knowing the trend for the month ahead can help to utilize the best days for success."

ART OF HORARY ASTROLOGY, DeLong. $15.00p AFA.

ART OF JUDGING TRANSITS, Terrye Lang. $8.25p ISBN 0-914350-51-X, VUL80. With case studies, the author teaches how to synthesize transiting planets with the natal horoscope.

ART OF SYNTHESIS, Alan Leo. $6.95p ISBN 0-89281-178-1, 318pp. INT/WEI68. This text offers valuable insights into the relationship between the planets and consciousness. Leo stresses esoteric and intuitional factors along with the philosophical and psychological aspects of astrology. He also discusses planetary correlations to temperament types with the aid of graphic illustrations.

ASCENDANT—YOUR KARMIC DOORWAY, Martin Schulman. $5.95p WEI. Mr. Schulman believes that the Ascendant is the expression of an individual's reality and that it becomes a doorway of understanding reality through one's essence. The book discusses karma, individuality, overcoming negativity, the Ascendant and nodes and gives an in-depth look at each Ascendant of the zodiac.

ASCENDING SIGN, E.C. Mathews. $4.50p 125pp. MOT70. This book contains one hundred forty-four portraits and profiles of the twelve Ascendant types with character analyses and vocational suggestions. The ascending signs of three hundred thirty-three famous people are analyzed. No prior knowledge of chart erection is necessary to use the folding chart supplied for finding ascending signs.

ASPECTS AND THEIR MEANINGS: Astro-Kinetics Vol 3, Edward W. Whitman. $8.00c ISBN 0-85243-171-6, 178pp. FOW70. This final volume of a series shows the reader the method for sight recognition of various aspects, making simple a procedure which often appears complicated. It includes a detailed description of the influence of the progressed Moon and of the progressed aspects of this luminary.

ASPECTS AT A GLANCE, Epstein. $5.00p WEI. In order to develop familiarity with a chart and synthesize the aspects, they must be easily discernable. This book teaches the beginning student how to see aspects in a chart by sign. Self-published with many illustrations.

ASPECTS BETWEEN SIGNS, Sophia Mason. $4.00p 74pp. MAS. Mason emphasizes "understanding the psychological and external influence on aspects between signs containing these planetary positions."

ASPECTS MAGNIFIED, Mohan Koparkar. $3.95p ISBN 0-918922-06-2, 78pp. MOH78. In this text, each major, minor and little known aspect is studied and analyzed for its qualities. The process of "magnification" is used to derive substantial delineations for these aspects. The meaning and uses of the minute aspects are given special attention.

ASPECTS TO HOROSCOPE ANGLES, Vivia Jayne. $6.00p 53pp. ASB74. Jayne's twenty years of astrological research into rectification of the horoscope angles is documented in her innovative conclusions about aspects to the Ascendant, Midheaven and vertex. She illustrates her presentation with many examples.

A SPIRITUAL APPROACH TO ASTROLOGY, Myrna Lofthus. $12.50c ISBN 0-533-0394-0-01, 428pp. VAN80. The planets, houses and zodiac signs are explained, and simple forms are provided for casting natal horoscopes. Chart interpretation from the mundane to the spiritual is discussed as well as progression of the natal chart and the meaning of aspect combinations. Psychic predictions are given on the influence of the outer planets in the years ahead.

ASTEROIDS IN MIDPOINTS, ASPECTS & PLANETARY PICTURES, Emma Donath. $16.00p 204pp. EDO/AFA81. Donath locates and identifies the three thousand six hundred midpoints of each of the four asteroids in midpoint to every known planet and personal point. For the cosmobiological and Uranian astrologer.

ASTEROIDS IN SYNASTRY, Emma Donath. $6.50p 95pp. EDO/AFA77. "Synastry or the astrology of relationships, principles or keywords for placement of the asteroids Ceres, Pallas, Athena, Juno, and Vesta in chart comparison, in the composite chart, in natal and progressed charts and who acts upon whom." The many sample charts that illustrate this study are discussed with an emphasis on practical application.

ASTEROIDS IN THE BIRTH CHART, Emma Donath. $4.00p 104pp. EDO/AFA79. The author asserts that Gemini's true rulers are the four main asteroids. The meanings of the asteroids in each of the signs and houses is clarified with keywords and sample charts.

ASTEROIDS IN THE U.S.A., Emma Donath. $9.80p 144pp. EDO/AFA79. Includes investigative techniques; charts for Jamestown and Plymouth settlements; horoscopes of forty-two United States vice-presidents; Ayanamsha tables for 1700-2010; asteroids as vocational indicators; historical charts with asteroid placements; analysis of American astronauts, cosmonauts, feminists, musicians, engineers, etc.

ASTRAL MEDICINE AND THERAPEUTICS, Dr. M. Duz. $5.00s facsimile reprint (1912) 252pp. HEA. Dr. Duz examines the relationship of astrology, biochemistry, homeopathy and diet using many diagrams.

ASTRO-CYCLES & SPECULATIVE MARKETS, L.J. Jensen. $25.00c 142pp. LAG78. Jensen has been able to predict the highs and lows of the stock and commodity markets by astrologically forecasting the time of natural events which affect the markets such as wars, weather, social trends, famines, earthquakes and business cycles. There are dozens of charts and graphs to support the author's research.

ASTRO-DIAGNOSIS: A GUIDE TO HEALING, Max Heindel and Augusta Foss Heindel. $5.00p 446pp. ROS29. Several astrological charts are used to illustrate how scientific knowledge regarding disease and its cause is shown by the planets as well as natural therapies. A chapter is devoted to each of the different parts of the body with instructions for diagnosing disease in the chart. This is particularly useful to those in health professions, whether orthodox or holistic in approach.

ASTRO-ECONOMICS, David Williams. $3.00p ISBN 0-87542-882-7, 54pp. LLE74. Williams establishes the theory that conjunctions and oppositions of Jupiter, Saturn and Uranus exert either a stabilizing or disturbing influence on the economy. For example, Saturn-Uranus conjunctions are associated with low periods in American business activity. Correlations are made between business activity and Sidereal patterns.

ASTROGIFTS, Mercedes Cortazar. $5.95p ISBN 0-06-090798-3, 192pp. HAR79. An innovative approach to choosing and giving presents. Astrogiving is based on understanding the twelve zodiacal personality types. The book includes an index to specific gift possibilities for both home-made and store bought gifts, including brand names and sources. The important moment and appropriate manner in which to give the gift is also discussed according to Sun-sign types.

ASTROLOGER LOOKS AT MURDER, Barbara Watters. $1.95p 173pp. AFA69. The author analyzes six of the most sensational murder cases ever: Jack the Ripper, Lizzie Borden, Halls-Mills, etc. Each case makes absorbing reading by itself and all are enhanced by astrological detective work which uncovers factors essential to the true understanding of the crimes.

ASTROLOGER ON WHEELS, Jack Provenzano. $15.95 16pp. AWH. 12"x12". Six sign-align wheels make charts and give readings using the Sun sign and year of birth for any day, month or year. Instructions are included.

ASTROLOGER'S CASEBOOK, Zipporah P. Dobyns and Nancy Roof. $4.00p 142pp. TIA. Designed for serious students who are already working with charts and seek a deeper psychological insight into the uses of the horoscope as a diagnostic tool.

ASTROLOGER'S CONDENSED MANUAL, T. Patrick Davis. $5.00p 53pp. DAV. This unique condensation of information is suitable for classroom use or for the self-taught student.

ASTROLOGERS GUIDE, William Lily. $3.75p. AFA.

ASTROLOGER'S GUIDE TO THE HARMONICS, James and Ruth Williamsen. $17.95p 435pp. AFA75. The companion piece to HARMONICS IN ASTROLOGY, this catalog of harmonics comes with guidelines for application. The authors include examples, explanations, a bibliography and a listing of sixteen hundred harmonics which are indexed and cross-tabulated.

ASTROLOGER'S NODE BOOK, Donna van Toen. $5.95p ISBN 0-87728-521-7, 128pp. WEI81. The author discusses the Nodes through all the signs and houses, outlining the problems inherent in each nodal position as well as the possible reasons for the problems, solutions and observations. She also covers aspects to the Nodes.

ASTROLOGER'S NOTEBOOK ON ASPECTS OF THE TRANSITING PLANETS, Mary Elsnau. $4.00p 92pp. HEA62. Basic information on transits is simply presented. The author highlights the spiritual aspects of astrology and provides blank pages for the reader's observations and experiences with transits.

ASTROLOGICAL ASPECTS, Charles E.O. Carter. $3.75p ISBN 8543-003-5, 160pp. FOW30. Carter, a noted British astrologer of the Margaret Hone school, delineates thirty-six possible combinations of the Sun, Moon and the seven known planets under three headings: harmonious aspects, the conjunction, and inharmonious aspects.

ASTROLOGICAL CHARACTERISTICS AND CONSCIOUSNESS OF THE 12 SIGNS OF THE ZODIAC, compilation. $4.00 109pp. HEA65. Each sign's ruling planet, color, perfume, metal, element, best location to live, part of body influenced most, best profession, musical tone, flower, gem, Biblical references, mineral salt and temperament. The author asserts that awareness of this information can help one develop a stronger personality.

ASTROLOGICAL CHART, GRAPHIC, $1.50 ROS. 22" x 15". This chart graphs the positions of Saturn, Uranus, Neptune and Pluto for years 1800 to 2000.

ASTROLOGICAL CHART OF THE UNITED STATES: FROM 1776 to 2141, Gar Osten. $10.00c ISBN 0-8128, 272pp. STE76. Using the Gemini-rising United States chart and planetary transits from 1776 to 2141, Osten studies the history of the United States in detail and speculates on future events. Both historical events and major planetary configurations are studied and presented chronologically. Example charts are used.

ASTROLOGICAL COMPATABILITY, Lynne Palmer. $9.50p AFA76. Palmer offers a variety of chart comparison techniques and concentrates on determining the positive and negative aspects in the interrelationship of two natal charts. She demonstrates the different techniques, giving technical instructions and case studies.

ASTROLOGICAL CYCLES AND THE LIFE CRISIS PERIODS, John Townley. $2.95p 51pp. WEI77. This study of cycles deals with diurnal, solar, lunar, planetary and non-astrological cycles in the overall life cycle as the foundation of all prediction.

ASTROLOGICAL ESSAYS, Ivy M. Goldstein-Jacobson. $9.00p GOJ. This volume stresses delineation and offers new approaches to natal chart reading. Included are a personal autobiography, a special presentation of Uranian astrology made easy, and a full illustrated description of the trans-Neptunian planets with keywords. Other topics include horary houses, parallel midpoints and much more.

ASTROLOGICAL FAMILY PATTERNS, Ruth Armstrong. $11.95p ISBN 0-02788-0-X, 137pp. CMD79. An analysis of the patterns and interchart relationships of twelve family groups, this study presents the kind of detailed and relevant research demanded by contemporary astrologers.

ASTROLOGICAL FORMS, Aquarian Book Publishers. $2.00 AQB. 8 1/2" x 11". This large eight inch wheel has a place for everything needed for a complete horoscope. The instructions provided on the reverse side show how to carry out the math needed to determine the placements of signs and the planets, including a logarithm table with instructions on how to use logarithms. A natural zodiac showing the signs in the heavens and their rulers. Pads of 52 each.

ASTROLOGICAL HOUSES: The Spectrum of Individual Experience, Dane Rudhyar. $2.95p ISBN 0-385-03827-5, 208pp. DOU72. Rudhyar examines the twelve houses in detail considering their meaning, origin and interpretation in the chart. He considers the houses the basic astrological frame of reference. Rudhyar's writing is humanistic, individualized and mentally stimulating.

ASTROLOGICAL INSIGHTS, Dane Rudhyar. $5.95p ISBN 0-88231-068-2, 160pp. ASI79. Rudhyar's penetrating and poetic insight into the twelve qualities required for spiritual life is based on the symbolism of the astrological signs and houses. He shows how to use basic life challenges as opportunities for personal evolution and change. Twelve artistic renderings evoke the archetypal, intuitive level of each sign.

ASTROLOGICAL INSIGHTS INTO PERSONALITY, Betty Lundsted. $9.95p ISBN 0-917086-22-8, 352pp. AST80. This book combines principle and practice. The author discusses each of the major planetary aspects as a context for personality development and presents chart analysis and synthesis. She asserts that the symbols in a natal chart illustrate childhood environment which can influence future expectations, relationships, self-esteem, sexuality and evolution.

ASTROLOGICAL INSIGHT TO YOUR KARMA, Margaret L. Grahek. $6.95c ISBN 0-533-03645-3, 96pp. VAN80. This book is about karmic theory, transmigration and astrology. It shows how to determine one's karmic lessons from the karmic chart and the twelve karmic houses, and offers paradigms for "correct living" to help develop and maintain a balanced karma.

ASTROLOGICAL JUDGMENT OF DISEASES, Nicholas Culpeper. $4.50p 135pp. AFA. Culpeper, a seventeenth century English physician and writer, is known for his HERBAL. This major work on astrological indications of disease is now issued as an offset reprint. He cites many case histories and instances to illustrate his material.

ASTROLOGICAL KEYS TO SELF REALIZATION & SELF ACTUALIZATION, Clara Weiss. $4.95p ISBN 0-87728-509-8, 128pp. WEI80. Based on the work of Madame Blavatsky and Alice Bailey, this book explores the esoteric significance of the astrological signs.

ASTROLOGICAL KEY TO BIBLICAL SYMBOLISM, Ellen McCaffery. $7.95c 192pp. WEI75. This book correlates religious symbolism and astrology. Hindu, Buddist and kabbalistic philosophies are included. The author covers initiation by Air, Fire, Earth, Water and discusses the religious symbolism of the signs.

ASTROLOGICAL ORIGINS, Cyril Fagan. $2.95p ISBN 0-87542-220-9, 224pp. LLE73. Fagan gives the history of sidereal astrology used by the ancients and asserts its superiority over tropical astrology. A lifetime study and research is documented in this account which includes instructions for converting a tropical chart to a sidereal one.

ASTROLOGICAL PATTERNS: The Key to Self Discovery, Frances Sakoian and Betty Caulfield. $12.95c ISBN 0-06-013779-7, 315pp. HAR80. Astrological patterns are recurrent systems that act upon and serve as clues to a person's character. Included are hemisphere patterns, mental chemistry patterns, natural disposition patterns, temperament type patterns and dynamic focus patterns. This is a guidebook to the interpretation of the planetary influences on the individual psychological makeup.

ASTROLOGICAL SIGNATURES, C.C. Zain. $7.50p ISBN 0-87887-345-7, 288pp. CHU73. Reincarnation, mundane houses, the zodiac and other subjects are examined in light of their relationship to the nature of the soul's progression, purpose and eventual form.

ASTROLOGICAL SIGNS: The Pulse of Life, Dane Rudhyar. $3.50p ISBN 0-394-73577-3, 144pp. SHA70. In this concise explanation of basic astrological principles, Rudhyar integrates the symbolism of the twelve signs with concepts in humanistic psychology.

ASTROLOGY, Ronald Davison. $.95p ISBN 0-668-01128, 175pp. ARC63. Davison gives definitions of the most important astrological concepts and directions for erecting a natal horoscope.

ASTROLOGY, Louis MacNeice. $6.95c ISBN 0-385-12212-8, 351pp. DOU64. This historical survey of astrology also doubles as an introductory textbook on the planets, signs and chart erection. The appendix contains sidereal time tables, simplified tables of houses and ephemerides. Many drawings and photographs, in both black-and-white and color, illustrate the book.

ASTROLOGY, A COSMIC SCIENCE, Isabel M. Hickey. $13.95c 280pp. HIC70. Isabel Hickey's basic and inspiring textbook emphasizes karmic and reincarnational astrology. She explains and interprets the planets, aspects and Moon's nodes by sign and house. The meanings of the signs on the cusps, medical astrology, chart calculation, transits and progressions are discussed.

ASTROLOGY AND HEALTH, Sheila Geddes. $6.95p. ISBN 0-85030-248-X, 128pp. WEI81. Each zodiacal sign is analyzed to show the psychological tendencies that may manifest as certain illnesses. There is a comprehensive reference section on prevention and treatment by natural therapies.

ASTROLOGY AND HEALTH, Sheila Geddes. $7.00p ISBN 0-85030-248-X, 128pp. AQU81. Analyzes each zodiacal sign to show the psychological tendencies that may manifest as illness and shows how to prevent these through a wide variety of natural therapies, from aromatherapy to radionics.

ASTROLOGY AND HERBS, Joan M. Harmon. $7.50p 120pp. ASA. Devoted to astrological identification of potential diseases and a review of herbs that have been reported to be beneficial in the treatment of such problems.

ASTROLOGY AND LOVE, Sybil Leek. $1.95p BER.

ASTROLOGY AND REINCARNATION, Manly Palmer Hall. $1.75p ISBN 0-89314-303-0, 45pp. PHR36. This publication contains three of Hall's essays: How to Read Your Past and Future Lives, Astrology and Reincarnation, and Astrology and Karma.

ASTROLOGY AND REINCARNATION: Vol 1: Retrograde Planets and Reincarnation, Donald Yott. $3.95p ISBN 0-87728-374-5, 94pp. WEI77. Yott's delineations of retrograde planets through the cycle of houses reflect the view that retrogrades are a focus for self-development. His writing is based on the pioneering work of Alice Fowler who taught that retrogrades indicate negative character traits brought on from previous incarnations.

ASTROLOGY AND REINCARNATION: Vol 2: Intercepted Signs and Reincarnation, Donald Yott. $3.50p ISBN 0-87728-374-5, 55pp. WEI77. The author develops his position that intercepted signs reveal qualities undeveloped in past lives. He examines zodiacal oppositions in all the houses and explains how to make positive adjustments in this lifetime.

ASTROLOGY AND REINCARNATION: Vol 3: Triangulation of Saturn, Jupiter and Mercury, Donald Yott. $3.50p ISBN 0-87728-394-X, 92pp. WEI79. In this concluding volume in the series, the author describes the relationships between

Saturn, Jupiter and Mercury and how they symbolize aspects of karma and reincarnation. He also discusses the karmic significance of Saturn in each of the twelve houses.

ASTROLOGY AND RELIGION AMONG THE GREEKS AND ROMANS, Franz Cumont. $2.75p ISBN 0-486-20581-9, 112pp. DOV12. This is a scholarly reconstruction of the Babylonian origin of astrology in the eighth century B.C. The author examines the impact of Chaldean astronomy, star worship and odd Near Eastern cults and mysteries on the history and development of early Greek, Roman, Syrian and Egyptian astrology.

ASTROLOGY AND ROMANCE, Elsbeth Ebertin. $7.95c ISBN 0-88231-002-X, 132pp. ASI26. This recent reprint of a 1926 classic treatise on synastry, or chart comparison, presents many astrological observations, both ancient and modern, with rules of interpretation. Over twenty horoscopes illustrate the author's research into relationships. The author gives interpretations of seventh-house planets and delineations of Sun-Moon combinations, with a view of the prospects for many kinds of relationships.

ASTROLOGY AND SEXUAL ANALYSIS, Morris C. Goodman. $7.50c ISBN 0-8303-0094-5, FLE. Interpretations and a compatibility guide for both males and females born under each sign, with a frank, illuminating analysis of the individual's sexual likes and dislikes, freedoms and hang-ups, talents and handicaps, thoughts, dreams, fantasies and erotic secrets. The book is illustrated with reproductions of classic works of erotic art by such masters as Gauguin, Rodin, Fragonard and Dore.

ASTROLOGY AND STOCK MARKET FORECASTING, Louise McWhirter. $17.50c ISBN 0-88231-034-8, 244pp. ASI77. The author combines her specialties by originating this theory of stock market forecasting. This book is a source of techniques and information on financial astrology, and is of value to both students of astrology and economic analysts.

ASTROLOGY AND THE DUCTLESS GLANDS, Augusta Foss Heindel. $1.00p 34pp. ROS. This study gives astrological rulers of the different ductless glands and indicates their functions. The contents include Polarian Epoch, the Garden of Eden, Two Ductless Glands and the Spinal Gas.

ASTROLOGY AND THE EDGAR CAYCE READINGS, Margaret Gammon. $2.50p 78pp. ARE74. The astrological material selected from Edgar Cayce's readings covers the "Akashic Records," soul evolution, cusps, transits, cycles, and the planets as experiences between incarnations and as specific influences on Earth lives.

ASTROLOGY AND THE FEMINIST MOVEMENT, Robert Carl Jansky. $8.00p 158pp. ASA77. A guide to basic chart delineation using as examples charts of the fifty most famous women in the Feminist Movement. Jansky traces the history of the movement from its earliest days to the present, adding interesting historical perspective to delineation techniques.

ASTROLOGY AND THE I CHING, Wen Kuan Chu. $9.95p ISBN 0-87728-492-X, 451pp. WEI76. This translation of a classical Chinese manuscript gives complete instructions for making predictions by combining the I Ching and astrology. By using the charts, diagrams and tables provided, astrological time sequences are translated into the symbolism of the I Ching. The author offers his own interpretations of the ancient hexagrams as they affect ordinary people in personal and professional situations.

ASTROLOGY AND THE MODERN PSYCHE, Dane Rudhyar. $5.95p ISBN 0-916360-05-9, 182pp. CRC76. In a series of articles, the author introduces the student of astrology to the pioneers of psychological thought in this century: Freud, Adler, Jung, Kunkel, Moreno and Assagioli, relating their ideas to astrology and to their own birth charts. Rudhyar, the foremost psychological astrologer of our time, examines the self and the ego in relation to the planets and their functions in the human psyche.

ASTROLOGY AND THE TAROT, A.E. Thierens. $3.95p ISBN 0-87877-031-3; $9.95c ISBN 0-87877-331-2, 159pp. NCP75. Astrological correspondences to the Tarot are made as the author discusses the esoteric meanings of the individual minor arcana cards, the suits and the more often discussed major arcana cards.

ASTROLOGY FOR AND ABOUT YOUNG PEOPLE, Sue Ann. $9.95p. ISBN 0-960-04172-0-6, 177pp. SUE80. Using an elementary teacher's techniques, the author presents an easy approach to basic astrology. She employs language and terminology appropriate for young people without oversimplification.

ASTROLOGY FOR DOGS (AND OWNERS), William Fairchild. $8.95p ISBN 0-241-10380-0, 95pp. HAM80. The characteristics of dogs born under each sign are explained along with a list of do's and don't's for owners, the respective compatible human signs and possible health problems. Fredrick Davoes has written the foreword and famous dog owners like Barbara Cartland and Alec Guinness add their experiences.

ASTROLOGY FOR EVERYDAY LIVING, Janet Hartis. $3.00p ISBN 0-87980-007-0, 192pp. WIL61. This book uses astrology to show how each person's destiny and personality is unique. It shows how to lead a happy and successful life by identifying and developing one's talents and potentialities.

ASTROLOGY FOR THE AQUARIAN AGE, Alexandra Mark. $4.95p ISBN 0-671-21678-3, 400pp. SIM70. Instructions are given for erecting solar and natal charts with interpretations for the signs, aspects and houses.

ASTROLOGY FOR THE NEW AGE, Marcus Allen. $4.95p ISBN 0-931432-03-0, 127pp. WHA77. A unique and refreshing approach to astrology that shows how to apply the teaching of this ancient science to today's individual patterns of personal growth and evolution.

ASTROLOGY GUIDE TO YOUR SEX LIFE, Vivian Robson. $.95p ISBN 0-668-01628-0, 140pp. ARC63. The sex life of men and women is explored in an astrological context. Seven horoscope charts are used as case studies, including Oscar Wilde and Tchaikovsky.

ASTROLOGY: How to Chart Your Horoscope, Max Heindel. $3.00p ISBN 0-87980-005-4, 198pp. WIL28. This textbook presents a simplified method for erecting a horoscope. With the many tables provided, only knowledge of addition and subtraction is required.

ASTROLOGY IN ACTION, Marcia Moore and Mark Douglas. $7.00c ISBN 0-912240-03-2, 336pp. ARN70. The application of astrology is illustrated by means of astrotypes, keywords, forty-two horoscopes and methods of predicting the future. There are comparisons of Jacqueline Kennedy Onassis' horoscope with those of John F. Kennedy and Aristotle Onassis, a study of the death aspects of the Kennedy brothers, horoscopes and profiles of the family.

ASTROLOGY IN A NUTSHELL, Prof. C.H. Webber. $5.00s fascimile reprint (1902) 132pp. HEA.

ASTROLOGY INSIDE OUT, Bruce Nevin. $9.95p ISBN 0-914918-19-2, 300pp. PAR81. This is a modern introduction to astrology and much more. Even before looking at a horoscope, the reader learns to translate personal experiences into the symbol-language of astrology. Through visualization and meditation exercises, even seasoned astrologers will gain new appreciation of astrological patterning from the "inside out."

ASTROLOGY IN THE BUFF, Mary A. Letorney. $5.95p 153pp. PRA80. The twelve Sun signs are interpreted clearly and simply.

ASTROLOGY: ITS TECHNIQUES, C.A. Libra. $3.95p ISBN 0-87877-035-6; $9.95c ISBN 0-87877-335-5, 271pp. NCP76. This recently reprinted classic text covers the basics but also includes material for the advanced student. It has a strong spiritual quality and communicates religious concepts and karmic theory. The delineations have the negative tone which is so prevalent in the older texts.

ASTROLOGY, KARMA AND TRANSFORMATION, Stephen Arroyo. $7.95p ISBN 0-916360-03-2; $10.95c ISBN 0-916360-04-0, 250pp. CRC78. An original book focusing on astrology as a tool for spiritual and psychological growth. Arroyo departs from "prediction" and concentrates on the direction of self-transformation.

ASTROLOGY, KEY TO SELF UNDERSTANDING, Leonora Luxton. $4.95p ISBN 0-87542-331-0, 262pp. LLE78. This introductory work on spiritual astrology clarifies the relationship between karma, astrology and reincarnation. The author gives a method for evaluating the spiritual evolution of the soul and the progress achieved through former incarnations. She shows how knowledge of one's place in the universe can be known through a deep understanding on the birth chart.

ASTROLOGY-MUNDANE AND SPIRITUAL, S.R. Parchment. $4.00s facsimile reprint 906pp. HEA. An old-style astrology book that combines traditional astrological insights with mundane astrology.

ASTROLOGY, NUTRITION AND HEALTH, Robert Carl Jansky. $6.95p ISBN 0-914918-07-9 180pp. PAR77. Jansky explains how to use the natal horoscope to foresee and prevent health problems. The author is a professional astrologer trained in biochemistry and demonstrates how a knowledge of astrology can help the reader understand the components of metabolism and health.

ASTROLOGY OF ACCIDENTS, Charles E.O. Carter, $3.95p THE. The stars are used to determine the probability of accidents.

ASTROLOGY OFF THE TOP, Sydney Omarr. $5.00p AFA.

ASTROLOGY OF HUMAN RELATIONSHIPS, Frances Sakoian and Louis Acker. $12.95c ISBN 0-06-013712-6, 448pp. HAR76. An in-depth study of natal chart comparison. The influence of planets on paired relationships such as husband and wife, parent and child and business associates is discussed by house placement and aspect. The book reviews basic astrological principles and provides a glossary and an index.

ASTROLOGY OF PERSONALITY, Dane Rudhyar. $2.95p ISBN 0-385-06699-6, 50pp. DOU70. Rudhyar reexaminations old astrological concepts and ideas in an attempt to modernize astrology. Horoscope casting, interpretations, progressions and transits are all discussed.

ASTROLOGY OF RELATIONSHIP, Michael Meyer. $3.95p ISBN 0-385-11556-3, 263pp. DOU76. Meyer's humanistic approach to astrology is applied to this volume on synastry, an astrological technique which compares the birth charts of two or more persons to determine compatibility. He philosophically explains the significance of the planets, houses and signs in synastry and gives complete instructions for casting and interpreting house contact, zodiacal contact and composite charts.

ASTROLOGY OF SEXUALITY, Martin Schulman. $7.95p ISBN 0-87728-481-4, 176pp. WEI80. Schulman discusses the sexual interpretation of the horoscope through a careful study of the houses, house size, positive-negative qualities and planetary energies of the houses.

ASTROLOGY OF THE OLD TESTAMENT, Karl Anderson. $12.00s facsimile reprint 502pp. HEA. This was originally entitled THE LOST WORD REGAINED (1892 first edition). The book contains two large folded charts, many full page illustrations, tables of houses for latitude 55 degrees 53 minutes to latitude 63 degrees, and a table for turning degrees and minutes into time and for turning time into degrees and minutes.

ASTROLOGY OF TRANSCENDENCE, Philip Sedgewick. $10.95p ISBN 0-930706-06-4, 320pp. SEK80. The author takes modern discoveries and theories of astronomy and shows how they apply to astrological interpretations. Includes life cycles of Saturn and Uranus, the Moon's north node, black holes, galactic centers, solar apex and more.

ASTROLOGY OF TRANSFORMATION, Dane Rudhyar. $5.25p ISBN 0-8356-0542-6, 206pp. THE80. Rudhyar introduces a four-step approach to psychology and astrology. He defines the signs, the planets and the horoscope itself at each level of analysis. This guided adventure in self-examination presents Rudhyar's transpersonal approach to astrology and psycho-spiritual development.

ASTROLOGY, PALMISTRY, AND DREAMS, Donald Law. $2.95p ISBN 0-8226-0298-9, 160pp. LIT75. This book illustrates how a systematic analysis of signs, palmistry, intuition and science will make character reading and forecasting the future possible.

ASTROLOGY: PRACTICAL APPLICATION, Else Parker. $4.95p ISBN 0-87877-03909; $10.95c ISBN 0-87877-339-8, 204pp. NPC27. Reprinted from the 1927 original, this spiritually interpreted astrology text includes chapters on the planets, signs, houses, aspects, the planets in signs and houses, ascending signs, the Part of Fortune in houses and progressions.

ASTROLOGY, PSYCHOLOGY AND THE FOUR ELEMENTS, Stephen Arroyo. $5.95p ISBN 0-916360-01-6; $9.95c ISBN 0-916360-02-4, 250pp. CRC75. This first book by Arroyo deals with the relationship of astrology to modern psychology and with the use of astrology as a practical method for understanding one's attunement to universal forces. Part One of this book was awarded the 1973 Astrology Prize by the British Astrological Association.

ASTROLOGY REBORN, John Addey. $4.95p AFA. This is Addey's lecture on harmonics, contemporary science and the historical framework which unifies them, together with a 1975 postscript and bibliography by Dr. James Williamsen, Ph. D., (Cambridge Circle).

ASTROLOGY: Sense or Nonsense?, Roy A. Gallant. $6.95c ISBN 0-385-08673-3, 256pp. DOU74. The author, an astronomer, has written an objective, general account of astrology. He reviews the history of astrological practice and practitioners and gives some coverage to the meaning of the signs and planets. The book is profusely illustrated and includes a glossary and index.

ASTROLOGY SIMPLIFIED AND LIFE DELINEATOR, Lyman E. Stowe. $2.50p facsimile reprint 42pp. HEA. This book teaches how to cast a horoscope by the Universal System.

ASTROLOGY: SIMPLIFIED AND ILLUSTRATED, E.C. Mathews. $4.00p MOT. This basic book for classes and home study shows how to erect an accurate horoscope, find the aspects between planets and interpret astrological factors. Rulerships over various objects and affairs are assigned to the different planets, houses and signs.

ASTROLOGY, SIMPLIFIED SCIENTIFIC, Max Heindel and Augusta Foss Heindel. $3.00p; $4.50c 198pp. ROS. This is a complete textbook on fundamental astrology and the art of erecting a horoscope. Earnest students can instruct themselves in the mathematical details of astrology by using this volume which is written especially for beginners.

ASTROLOGY'S PEW IN CHURCH, Moby Dick. $10.00p 80pp. MOB. Religion and astrology are brought together in this analysis of every biblical reference to astrology. This research suggests that astrology is basic to Western civilization's rootstock Hebrew religion. An historically documented presentation of the natal charts of King David and Jesus are included.

ASTROLOGY: The Celestial Mirror, Warren Kenton. $5.00p ISBN 0-500-81004-4, 128pp. THA74. The historical development and its applications are presented in this pictorial study including thirty outstanding color and one hundred sixteen black-and-white prints.

ASTROLOGY: THE DIVINE SCIENCE, Marcia Moore and Mark Douglas. $20.00c ISBN 0-912240-04-0, 850pp. ARN71. The authors present astrology in a readable manner that enables the reader to understand basic character, human relationships and life-trends. The book contains all the information for becoming an expert astrologer and includes instructions for casting and interpreting horoscopes.

ASTROLOGY, THE SACRED SCIENCE, Joan Hodgson. $7.95p ISBN 0-85487-045-8; $12.95c ISBN 0-85487-042-3, 256pp. WHE/CRC78. An astrological discussion of the destiny of man and basic questions about life on Earth. The book describes the cosmic cycle by which souls incarnate, and the zodiacal and planetary influences which shape their characters, lives and bodies. A visionary account of the Aquarian Age and spiritual development through the ages is also given. It is for astrologers and meditators.

ASTROLOGY, 30 YEARS RESEARCH, Doris Chase Doane. $9.00p 303pp. AFA56. These findings are representative of the work done by Church of Light Research Department from 1924 to 1954. The tabulations of planets, signs and aspects indicate individual predispositions to certain vocations, disease, travel, etc., based on their studies comparing natal charts and case histories. Stellar dynamics and a study of twenty-four major progressions of the United States natal chart are included.

ASTROLOGY: WORLDS VISIBLE AND INVISIBLE, Everett Blackman. $5.25p 94pp. AFA74. This recent work on mundane astrology focuses on presidents, cycles and progressions. The United States chart and several case studies are illustrated. The author discusses the presidency, presidents who have died in office and those who have succeeded such a president.

ASTROLOGY: Your Personal Sun-Sign Guide, Beatrice Ryder. $3.00p ISBN 0-87980-006-2, 224pp. WIL69. This astrology book requires no calculations, and is designed to delineate the character and provide readings without charts, pencil work or mathematics. The work is based on Sun-sign and decanate interpretations.

ASTROLOGY: YOUR WHEEL OF FORTUNE, Anthony Norvell. $3.50p ISBN 0-06-464008-6, HAR74. This book gives general information on the twelve Sun signs, and includes topics such as health, profession, love, children, wealth and destiny.

ASTRO-PALMISTRY, Cyrus D.F. Abavakoon. $20.00c ISBN 0-88231-012-7, 190pp. ASI75. Based on Hindu tradition, this method of interpretation deals with astrology and its relationship to the lines and shape of the hand. The presentation of case histories supports the correlating material found in horoscopes and palm prints.

ASTROPHYSICAL DIRECTIONS, Michael and Margaret Erlewine. $10.00p 140pp. SEK77. The Erlewines' spiritual perspective is strong in their analysis of the three coordinate systems that form the basis of astrology. They discuss the solar system, planets, asteroids and galactic nebulae. There are also tables that locate astronomical phenomena in the natal chart.

ASTRO-PSYCHOLOGY, Karen Hamaker-Zondag. $7.95p ISBN 0-87728-465-2, 224pp. WEI80. The traditional wisdom of astrology is examined in light of Jungian psychology. The author explores the astrological significance of Jung's terminology, including archetypes, the collective unconscious and the theory of synchronicity and concludes by emphasizing the correspondence between Jung's theories and traditional astrological symbolism.

ASTRORHYTHMS, Mary Orser and Rick and Glory Brightfield. $5.95p ISBN 0-06-090632-4, 160pp. HAR79. The authors' demonstrated method performs the same function as biorhythms to predict individual patterns of change. Nature's underlying cycles are an inherent basis of astrology and influence human behavior, energy patterns and activities. With the use of an astrology wheel, charts and diagrams, the authors have devised a system for plotting daily, weekly or longer personal cycles enabling people to plan their activities effectively.

ASTROSOPHIC PRINCIPLES, John Hazelrigg. $4.00p facsimile reprint (1917) 127pp. HEA. An enquiry into the tenets and the philosophy of the stellar science.

A TIME FOR ASTROLOGY, Jess Stearn. $2.50p ISBN 0-451-09363-1, 435pp. NEW71. Jess Stearn relates contemporary events to the charts of the United States and many of its presidents in this topical work. He incorporates an analysis of these charts, and those of other famous people in his discussion. In addition, he includes a partial ephemeris for 1900-1975, and tables for the position of the Moon and Ascendant.

AXE WAS GOD, Henry Binkley. $2.50 mimeographed 44pp. HEA. The jackal occupies the center of the zodiac.

AZTEC ASTROLOGY, K.C. Tunnicliffe. $8.80p ISBN 85243-358-1, FOW. This original work on a neglected subject includes material that many astrologers will not have encountered before.

BASIC FUNDAMENTALS OF THE NATAL CHART, Sophia Mason. $4.00p 78pp. MAS. Mason offers simple and clear step-by-step instructions for chart construction. This teaching guide also includes an ephemeris and a table of houses.

BASIS OF SCRIPTURE PROPHECY, Sepharial. $2.00s facsimile reprint HEA.

BEING A LUNAR TYPE IN A SOLAR WORLD, Donna Cunningham. $6.95p ISBN 0-87728-522-5, 176pp. WEI81. The author explores the mythical, magical and modern views of the Moon and its relationship to many functions from maternity to mothering.

BEST OF THE ILLUSTRATED NATIONAL ASTROLOGICAL JOURNAL, $11.95c 256pp. DEL. This compendium of articles and short stories appeared in the National Astrological Journal in 1933, 1934 and 1935. Contributing authors are Manly P. Hall, Robert DeLuce, L. Edward Johndro, Foss Heindel, Elbert Benjamine and more.

BOOK OF HOUSES, Robert Cole. $4.95p ISBN 0-934558-01-9; $8.95c ISBN 0-934558-04-3, 128pp. ENT80. The premise of this book is that people pass through a twelve-stage cycle of personality development every year. Each house and stage in the cycle is described. Prior knowledge of astrology is not necessary.

BOOK OF NODES AND THE PART OF FORTUNE, Ada Muir. $1.50p 46pp. MAC30. Delineates the nodes and Part of Fortune by sign and horoscope house and gives aspects and health indications. Consideration is also given to cusp conjunctions in progressed charts.

BOOK OF RETROGRADES, John McCormick. $5.00p 84pp. AFA75. The retrograde planets from 1880 to 1980 are graphically examined with the aid of four sets of tables. McCormick clarifies the meaning of a retrograde planet and gives interpretations for each planet in retrograde.

BOOK OF WORLD HOROSCOPES, Moon Moore. $15.00p 0-930706-04-8, 317pp. SEK80. Subtitled The Astrological Gazetteer of the Modern Geo-political World, this book contributes to the increasingly important field of mundane astrology. The introduction includes a discussion of key words relevant to geographical astrology for each planet. Charts and relevant astrological data are provided for all countries from Afghanistan to Zambia.

CARDINAL CROSS, William Davidson. $2.50p 20pp. AFA63. This is a transcript of one of Dr. Davison's lectures. He talks about the three cardinal crosses or grand square, the esoteric Doctrine of the Rays and evolutionary progress of the soul.

CAREER ASTROLOGY: Vocational Counceling for the 1980's, C. J. Puopinen. $8.95p ISBN 0-930840-10-0, 240pp. NIN80. This comprehensive system matches personalities (as analyzed through the horoscope) to the responsibilities and environment of occupations. It includes all major career fields with emphasis on areas which encourage personal development.

CASANOVA'S BOOK OF NUMBERS AND THE DAILY HOROSCOPE, trans. Jerzy Laskowski. $4.25p VUL.

CASENOTES OF A MEDICAL ASTROLOGER, Margaret Millard. $7.95p ISBN 0-87728-484-9, 208pp. WEI 80. Dr. Millard applies both her medical experience and her extensive astrological knowledge in this contemporary analysis of her patient's birth charts. This study, based on accurate birth data and first hand knowledge of medical symptoms and conditions, fills a gap in existing astrological study of disease and shows how medical astrology can be used for diagnosis and prevention of disease.

CASE STUDIES IN HORARY ASTROLOGY, Joan Titsworth. $5.00p 62pp. ASA75. The author begins with a discussion of how to locate a horary question by employing one of the twelve houses in a chart. She focuses on two case studies accompanied by questions for each house, the circumstances surrounding the question and a detailed interpretation of the horary chart.

CASTING THE HOROSCOPE, Alan Leo. $6.95p ISBN 0-89281-176-5, 384pp. INT/WEI69. Leo teaches everything one needs to know to cast a natal chart, including calculation of the Ascendant, the use of the table of houses, how to read an ephemeris, the conversion of birthtime to sidereal time, and adjustments of planetary motions. For the more advanced student, there is information on rectification, directions, methods of house division, lessons in astronomy, and sample tables.

CAT SUN SIGNS, Vivian Buchan. $5.95p ISBN 0-8128-6097-7; $8.95c ISBN 0-8128-2686-8, 156pp. STE81. The author bases her work on the premise that cats' personalities are influenced by the planets too. The book is written for cat-lovers to show them how cats want and deserve to be treated.

CELEBRITY HOROSCOPES II, Angela Louise Gallo and J. Robert Prete. $5.00p 104pp. CHM75. This book contains biographical information, photographs and horoscope charts of movie and television stars, politicians, psychics and more. The charts were calculated using birth certificates or rectification when birthtime was unknown.

CELESTIAL DYNAMICS, Anonymous. $2.00 107pp. HEA. A course of astro-metaphysical study.

CELESTIAL GARDENING, Carole DeMott. $2.95p 50pp. COS80. The Moon's daily sign placement is used to determine the appropriate days for sowing, harvesting and other gardening activities. Also included is a table of Moon positions for 1981 through 1985.

CELESTIAL HARMONY: A Guide to Horoscope Interpretation, Martin Schulman, $7.95p ISBN 0-87728-495-4, 176pp. WEI80. This guide to horoscope interpretation covers planetary rulerships, decanates and duads, elements, mystical cycles, detriment, fall and exaltation.

CERTAIN FUNDAMENTALS OF ASTROLOGY, Johannes Kepler. $1.25p 31pp. CLA.

CHART OF DESTINY, Lyman E. Stowe. $1.50 HEA. 11" x 17" card stock. Chart of the astrologer's guide to the fixed stars.

CHART RECTIFICATION, Doris V. Thompson. $7.00p 129pp. AFA. Thompson gives simple step-by-step instructions for chart rectification. Several techniques defining events timed by progressions and transits are illustrated.

CHART YOUR OWN STARS, Doris V. Thompson. $24.95c 264pp. MAC. Learning to set up a natal chart has been the stumbling block of many potential astrologers. This well-illustrated book guides the new or reluctant astrologer each step of the way in erecting a chart for any birthtime and birthplace. A test chart is included.

CHEIRO'S WHEN WERE YOU BORN, Cheiro. $.95p ISBN 0-668-01168-8, ARC.

CHURCH OF LIGHT RESEARCH AND REFERENCE CYCLOPEDIA, Vol 1, C.C. Zain. $7.50p ISBN 0-87887-330-9, 650pp. CHU72; CHURCH OF LIGHT RESEARCH AND REFERENCE CYCLOPEDIA, Vol 2, C.C. Zain. $7.50p ISBN 0-87887-331-7, 650pp. CHU72. Designed for the advanced student, this reference work is the result of studying more than five thousand natal and progressed charts. Zain suggests different ways to delineate charts and he supplies a great deal of statistical and technical information.

CIRCLE BOOK OF CHARTS, Stephen Erlewine. $11.95p 275pp. AFA72. Erlewine's book contains the charts of over thirteen hundred leading figures of western civilization from Greece to the present. The charts are arranged chronologically and indexed alphabetically and by birthdate.

COFFEE TABLE BOOK OF ASTROLOGY, editor, John Lynch. $7.95p ISBN 0-14-004242-3, 326pp. PEN67. The bulk of this profusely illustrated compilation of writings on astrology consists of an analysis of the signs compiled from the writings of Alan Leo and Isabelle Pagan with an essay on spiritual astrology by Zoltan Mason and a section relating palmistry to astrology. It is prefaced by Lynch's history of astrology and study of the planets, and ends with a table of Ascendants and a 1900-1974 ephemeris of the Moon.

COMPARISONS, Clara M. Darr. $5.75p 48pp. DAR73. The author illustrates how the planets of another individual's chart affect you by falling into your natal houses. Material on transits and romance supplement her previous work entitled TRANSITS.

COMPLETE METHOD OF PREDICTION, Robert DeLuce. $8.75p ISBN 0-88231-027-5, 212pp. ASI35. This influential work on progressed horoscopes includes methods of directing, extensive interpretation of planetary arcs and mundane aspects, plus many useful mathematical and astronomical tables. The author views astrology as a vehicle for spiritual growth.

COMPOSITE CHART: The Horoscope of a Relationship, John Townley. $2.50p 47pp. WEI74. Townley shows how to calculate and progress the composite chart by interpreting the mutual midpoints of two natal charts. Brief and to the point, the author illustrates his material with example charts including Nixon and the United States.

CONCEPT OF CYCLE IN MODERN SCIENCE, ASTROLOGY AND I CHING, Charles Graham. $6.95p AFA76. A synthesis between historical and contemporary concepts of structure and process. The unifying idea is that of harmonics.

CONJUNCTIONS: An In-Depth Delineation, Donald Yott. $6.95p ISBN 0-87728-524-1, 208 pp. WEI81. This book gives an in-depth delineation of all possible conjunctions in the horoscope. Yott believes in a narrow orb of 3 degrees and stresses the blending of influences when the planets are in conjunction.

CONTACT COSMOGRAM, Reinhold Ebertin. $8.00p 151pp. HBV74. The contact cosmogram, Ebertin's method of chart comparison, is based on the stellar positions at birth seen in relationship to particular events or current constellations. He demonstrates the contact cosmogram and graphically illustrates it with charts and discussion.

CONTEMPORARY ASTROLOGY, Jerry J. Williams. $7.95p ISBN 0-914918-31-1, 360pp. PAR81. Illustrated with diagrams, charts and drawings, this book will help the reader construct and interpret an astrological chart. This book presents the basics of astrology and encompasses psychology, metaphysics, mythology and politics.

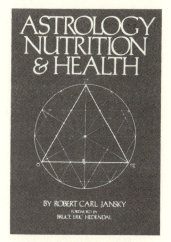

CONTEMPORARY WORLD HOROSCOPES: North and South America, S. Joseph Folino. $15.00c ISBN 0-88231-071-2, ASI80; CONTEMPORARY WORLD HOROSCOPES: Asia and Europe, $15.00c ISBN 0-88231-072-0, ASI80; CONTEMPORARY WORLD HOROSCOPES: Africa and Australia, $15.00c ISBN 0-88231-073-9, ASI81. A modern collection of over two hundred authenticated charts of nations, possessions, territories and dominions of the world. Each mundane chart is accompanied by a brief historical outline of the country. Appendices give the source of each chart used as well as listing the popular variations of disputed charts.

CONVERSE CHART, Whitcraft. $4.50p AFA.

CORNERSTONES OF ASTROLOGY, Gustave Schwickert and Weiss. $10.00p AFA.

COSMIC ALCHEMY, C.C. Zain. $7.50p ISBN 0-87887-351-1, 288pp. CHU46. Zain develops his philosophical position that humanity has an unfolding role of special significance in the universe and is not merely a disconnected intelligence.

COSMIC CLUES AND HELPFUL HINTS FOR HOROSCOPES, Doris V. Thompson. $5.00p 130pp. AFA. This is a compendium of astrological tidbits.

COSMIC INFLUENCES ON HUMAN BEHAVIOR, Michel Gauquelin. $8.95p 320pp. ASI73. Gauquelin documents a relationship between vocation and birth horoscopes based on his scientific study of twenty-five thousand European professionals listed in WHO'S WHO. He found that certain planets were found more frequently at the rising or culminating positions in the horoscope such as Mars in the case of athletes. The volume includes his latest findings on the planetary factors in personality.

COSMIC MARRIAGE, Reinhold Ebertin. $8.00p 160pp. HBV74. Ebertin explores synastry or astrological compatibility in-depth and documents his theories on cosmic marriage with many sample charts. He interprets the stellar positions by sign and examines their configurations with respect to fate and marital disposition. The significance of midpoints, major aspects and planetary activity in the house of marriage is analyzed. Directions for use of the ninety degree workboard are given.

COSMIC PATTERNS; Their Influence on Man and His Communication, John H. Nelson. $5.00p AFA. The author explains how heliocentric planetary aspects can predict interference in short-wave radio transmissions.

COUNSELING MANUAL IN ASTROLOGY, Marc Edmund Jones. $13.50c ISBN 0-87878-017-3, 224pp. AFA79. Jones describes the astrologer as at once a scientist and a creator, finding the freedom within the limitations of the discipline of astrology to be flexible and intuitive. Astrological counseling can be more meaningful says Jones, by focusing on fundamental metaphysical principles which apply to everyone. The macrocosm, which includes recurring principles in nature and man, is applied to the microcosm, the individual charts. Free will or the notion of unpredictability is also stressed.

CREATIVE REALITIES: Astrological Approaches to Self-Determination, John Scott Fisher. $5.50p 58pp. AFA. Fisher discusses major planetary patterns, opposition aspects, elements, qualities and more. His theme is that we create much of our own lives by how we react to situations.

CYCLE CHART, Lyman E. Stowe. $1.50 HEA. 8" x 7" card stock, revolving disc.

CYCLES OF BECOMING, Alexander Ruperti. $7.95p ISBN 0-916360-07-5, 288pp. CRC78. A penetrating treatment of transits from a humanistic and holistic perspective. All important planetary cycles are dealt with in depth and correlated with essential phases of personal developments.

CYCLIC ASTROLOGY, Irene Howell. $4.25p 68pp. DAR74. The point-of-self method is used to rectify and progress the birth chart, using three-year cycles of the Ascendant through the natal horoscope. Graphic examples illustrate the author's six years of research and experimentation.

DARK MOON LILITH IN ASTROLOGY, Ivy M. Goldstein-Jacobson. $7.50c 55pp. GOJ61. A comprehensive treatment of Earth satellite Lilith and her effect in natal, mundane, horary, prenatal and other charts. The author has also written an account of the origin and nature of this little understood and hard-to-see moon and provides an ephemeris from 1860 to 2000.

DAY OF YOUR BIRTH, Bernice Prill Grebner. $6.95p GRE81. This book gives a combined astrological and numerical delineation for your birthday that is not based on the month or the sign.

DAYS AND NIGHTS FOR MAKING LOVE: Sexual Timing with Astrology, Paul Rosner and Joyce Nunn. $12.95c ISBN 0-914350-39-0, 336pp. VUL. The authors claim that the "best" times for making love can be calculated in reference to individual birthdates. The system proposed is simple and easy to use.

DEDUCTIVE INTERPRETATION OF NATAL HOROSCOPE, John McCormick. $4.50p 68pp. AFA76. McCormick's review of the practical meanings of the planets, signs and houses is illustrated by demonstrating deductive interpretation in a lengthy case study. The author challenges traditional ideas and attempts to teach the student the inner meanings of the planets and their synthesis based on practical experience.

DEDUCTIVE INTERPRETATION OF THE PROGRESSED HOROSCOPE, John McCormick and Carol Rushman. $5.00p 118pp. AFA77. This monograph on the art of progressing horoscopes emphasizes McCormick's personal philosophy.

DEGREES OF LIFE, Chanda Dhi Manthri. $8.00p 98pp. ASA74. Manthri is deeply involved with the ancient Hindu and Egyptian schools of astrology and maintains that he found these degree readings in an old Sanskrit text. These poetic readings are substantially different from all others in print.

DEGREES OF THE ZODIAC, Esther V. Leinbach. $6.50p 189pp. MAC72. This practical guide to understanding the influence of the individual degrees is based on the author's own practical experience as an astrologer studying human behavior and from other leading authorities on the subject. The author asserts that as humanity matures the negative and violent degrees are showing more positive and useful expression.

DEGREES OF THE ZODIAC MAGNIFIED, Mohan Koparkar. $6.95p ISBN 0-918922-02-X, 217pp. MOH76. The author uses his technique of "magnification" to extract the significance of each degree of the zodiac, synthesizing house influences. The down-to-earth interpretations have a positive, psychologically-oriented quality.

DEGREES OF THE ZODIAC SYMBOLISED, Alan Leo. $3.50p ISBN 0-933646-01-1, 146pp. ARI. Charubel and Sepharial separate symbolism and interpretation for each of the three hundred sixty degrees in order to examine the degrees occupied by the Ascendant, Moon, Sun and ruling planet for sidelights on character and temperament. The Spiritual meaning derives from full use of intuition.

DEGREES OF THE ZODIAC SYMBOLISED, Charubel. $2.95p 135pp. ARI07. This reprint of an astrology manual by Alan Leo also includes Sepharial's translation of a series of esoteric descriptions of the degrees found in La Volasfera.

DEGREES OF THE ZODIAC SYMBOLIZED BY"CHARUBEL", Sepharial. $2.50 facsimile reprint (1907) 136pp. HEA.

DELINEATION OF MUNDANE EVENTS: The 90 Degree Disc Uranian Astrology, K. H. Ambjornson. $2.50p 22pp. KAM74. Two mundane events are completely delineated using the 90 degree disc technique. Included are all the mathematical calculations for all the planetary pictures used in these delineations. Complete illustrations with the planetary pictures as well as the horoscope wheel are given. The trans-Neptunian planets are emphasized.

DESTINY TURNS THE WHEEL, Hugh MacCraig. $4.50p 168pp. MAC. This guide to house-cusp interpretation shows how to interpret the natal or character chart and the destiny chart without mathematical calculations. The character chart shows the native's true type, disposition, desires and plans for life, and the destiny chart shows the native's challenges, true purpose in life and road to travel.

DEVIL'S PULPIT, Rev. Robert Taylor. $15.00s facsimile reprint (1882) 358pp. HEA. Contains 23 astronomico-theological discourses.

DIGESTED ASTROLOGER, Jinni Meyer and Joanne Wickenburg. $3.50p SEA. The material offered in this book is the digested and clarified wisdom of the greatest contemporary astrologers, researched by two astrology teachers who needed a complete reference for students. It is now being used by teachers throughout the United States and Canada as a required classroom text.

DIRECTIONS AND DIRECTING, H.S. Green. $2.00p 81pp. AFA72. Green gives"direction" on how to calculate, interpret and judge the effects of directions. Pre-natal directions, solar and lunar revolutions, transits and eclipses are included.

DISCRIMINATION OF BIRTHTYPES IN RELATION TO DISEASE, John Addey. $3.95p 25pp. AFA75. An exploration of startling facts, John Addey's extensive research in this area is analyzed and graphically illustrated in this technical monograph.

DISTANCE VALUES 1971-1980, Zipporah P. Dobyns. $1.50p 67pp. TIA72. Percentages are given based on the smallest and largest distances of the Sun, Moon, and planets from Earth for use in astrological research and chart interpretation. The introduction covers possible meanings and gives examples.

DIVINE LANGUAGE OF CELESTIAL CORRESPONDENCES, Coulson Turnbull. $6.00s 350pp. HEA. This study of planetary and spiritual vibrations and esoteric astrology gives an account of the involution and evolution of the soul. Chart making is also covered with tables of houses and astrological short-cuts.

DWADASHAMSAS: Degree Analyses and Deeper Meanings, John Sandbach. $6.00p 190pp. SEK78. This book explains in full detail the meanings for each 2 ½ degree segment of the zodiac known as the dwadashamsas. The author's method is based on ancient Chaldean astrology, which combines sign rulerships with numerological analysis.

EARTH AND THE HEAVENS, L. Edward Johndro. $6.95p WEI. Relates the precession of the equinoxes to the midheavens and ascendants of cities and shows the uses of locality angles in nativities.

EARTHOLOGY, HUMANITY CHARACTERIZED BY SUN, EARTH AND ZODIAC, Raphael. $5.00p facsimile reprint (1901) HEA. Prognostications from the Moon. Large folded chart.

ECLIPSES, Sepharial. $2.95p 112pp. SYM73/ASA. Sepharial applies all phases of the astrological significance and meaning of eclipses to individual and mundane affairs and charts.

ECLIPSES AND LUNATIONS IN ASTROLOGY, Sam Bartolet. $3.00p 60pp. AFA. This introductory volume on lunations and eclipses advises on correct procedures for applying lunations. The tables are both useful and interesting study material.

EIGHTH HOUSE, Marc Robertson. $3.95p 75pp. ACN76. This in-depth discussion of the eighth houses deals with sexual and monetary matters. Transit tables for timing investments are included.

ELECTIONAL ASTROLOGY, Christine Lorigan Rechter. $6.00p 59pp. ASA75. This textbook, which is designed for classroom use and lecturing, gives guidance and rules on setting up and interpreting the electional chart. This type of chart is used to locate the best time for an event or activity. It is illustrated by many case studies and example charts.

ELECTIONAL ASTROLOGY, Vivian Robson. $7.50c 228pp. WEI72. The author explains the general rules and principles for making and interpreting electional charts to find the best times for all undertakings, from a haircut to a wedding. The book covers business transactions, public and legal affairs, agriculture, gardening and much more. A glossary of terms and an index is also included.

ELEMENTS OF ASTROLOGY, Al-Biruni. $16.50c ISBN 0-88231-052-6, ASI80. The most important medieval work on Arabic Astrology.

ELEMENTS OF HOUSE DIVISION, Ralph W. Holden. $7.95p ISBN 85243-354-9, 157pp. FOW. The meaning of the houses in the horoscope, together with a comprehensive examination of the various methods of house division and its attendant problems. The text is given added depth by the inclusion of a resume of astrology's historical development.

ENCOUNTER ASTROLOGY, Maritha Pottenger. $5.00p TIA. Based on astrological themes, this collection of exercises allows the student to feel and experience traditional astrological meanings. The book is illustrated with dozens of photographs.

ENCYCLOPEDIA OF MEDICAL ASTROLOGY, H.L. Cornell. $20.00c 958pp. WEI72. This standard work presents a thoroughly indexed and cross-referenced text on medical astrology with a comprehensive, alphabetical listing of natural and pathological medical conditions. The planet, sign or luminary affecting or ruling each condition is given.

ENCYCLOPEDIA OF PSYCHOLOGICAL ASTROLOGY, Charles E.O. Carter. $5.95p ISBN 0-8356-5124-X; $9.95c ISBN 0-8356-5057-X, 199pp. THE63. A scientific approach is used in this work on personality and disease. Documented sources, such as nativities of royalty, are used to substantiate the author's findings.

ENGINE OF DESTINY, Marc Robertson. $5.50p 90pp. AFA. Robertson describes the eight personality types, reincarnation and the cycles of incarnation.

ESOTERIC ASTROLOGY, Alan Leo. $6.95p ISBN 0-89281-181-1, 320pp. INT/WEI67. The first of this book's three parts explains esoteric astrological theory; the second demonstrates its practical side, with many examples; the third deals with the subdivisions of the zodiac. A series of star maps are included which show how the age of the soul may be astrologically discovered. Chart interpretations are included for reincarnation and methods of resolving karma.

ESOTERIC ASTROLOGY, Alice Bailey. $15.00c 742pp. LUC51. Bailey believes the science of esoteric astrology is the basic occult science of the future. Astrology is described in this book as "the science of relationships," a science which deals with all universal energies and forces.

ESOTERIC ASTROLOGY: Past and Present Lives, Angela Louise Gallo. $3.50 27pp. CHM71. In order to determine the individual soul growth, the author explains how to find past lives and how these lives are pertinent to the present.

ESSAYS ON MEDICAL ASTROLOGY, Robert Carl Jansky. $8.00p 99pp. ASA80. In this collection of revised and expanded essays, Jansky covers the fundamentals of medical astrology, nutrition, fat metabolism and more. Comprehensive articles on Pluto's medical implications are also included.

ESSAYS ON THE FOUNDATIONS OF ASTROLOGY, Charles E.O. Carter. $5.95p; $9.95c THE65. A consideration of many fundamental questions with chapters on the Sun, Moon and planets. The author discusses aspects in terms of the signs and exaltations, the positive-negative polarity, the northern and southern signs and the houses.

ESSENCE OF SIDEREAL HINDU ASTROLOGY, Dorothy Robertson. $5.95p 188pp. BHA71. This book deals with the basics of sidereal Hindu astrology.

EVERY ASTROLOGER HAS BEEN THERE, Sandra Durst. Book I $3.85p; Book II $4.85p AFA. Durst offers a basic introduction to astrology and discusses different psychological stages, the changing astrological language and fees for astrologers.

EVERYTHING HAS A PHASE, Bernice Prill Grebner. $6.50p GRE80. This book is mostly about the the Moon: its phases through and in the signs, the astronomy of the Moon, the other side of the Moon, the pyschological and physical meaning of being a satellite, lunar returns and lunar mansions. It also contains the moons of other planets, asteroids, Lilith and what it really is, ages of man in relationship to the Moon and planets, time and the calendar, and more.

EVERYTHING YOU WANT TO KNOW ABOUT BLACK MAGIC, REVELATIONS BY ZOLAR, METAPHYSICAL ASTROLOGY, MEDIUMSHIP, CRYSTAL GAZING, Zolar. $.95p ISBN 0-668-02658-8, ARC.

EVOLUTIONARY ASTROLOGY: The Journey of the Soul Through the Horoscope, Raymond A. Merriman. $45.00c 230pp. SEK. This beautiful book is done in fine calligraphy with special inks and papers and is illustrated in both color and black-and-white prints. A psychological and metaphysical approach is taken to horoscope interpretation.

EVOLUTION THROUGH THE ZODIAC, Zipporah P. Dobyns. $1.50p 33pp. TIA72. Dobyns presents an astrological world-view that the essential meaning of the twelve Sun signs is a symbolic portrayal of man's spiritual evolution.

FINANCIAL ASTROLOGY TECHNIQUES, Boyd. $6.75p AFA.

FINDING THE PERSON IN THE HOROSCOPE, Zipporah P. Dobyns. $4.00p 63pp. TIA73. The humanistic point of view is taken in this analysis of selected astrological factors. The aspects, elements, midpoints, nodes, asteroids, fixed stars and Saturn are all part of this discussion of how the horoscope can be a mirror of personality, helping the native grow toward an infinite potential.

FIRST STEPS TO ASTROLOGY, Crowmarsh. $1.25p 64pp. WEI. This sixty-four page book on elementary astrology includes a brief analysis of the Sun signs, planets and aspects plus a chapter on health issues.

FIVE BOOKS OF MANILIUS, Manilius. $4.50p 179pp. AFA. 1697. Manilius' books, translated here by T.C., were written more than one hundred years before Ptolemy. They enlighten our understanding of Greek and Roman influence on astrology. The writings include all of the primary principles of modern astrology.

FIXED STARS AND CONSTELLATIONS IN ASTROLOGY, Vivian Robson. $5.95p ISBN 0-87728-232-3, 264pp. WEI69. This systematic compilation of astrological and astronomical material discusses the influence of the fixed stars and constellations in natal and mundane astrology.

FIXED STARS AND DEGREES OF THE ZODIAC ANALYZED, E.C. Mathews, $3.00p 76pp. MOT68. These readings for the three hundred sixty different degrees are based on an analysis of more than five hundred actual horoscopes. Each degree has a keyword or characteristic name, along with the delineation. Planetary natures and longitude of important stars in the signs are all written in simple language.

FOCUS ON NEPTUNE, Virginia Elenbaas. $6.00p 144pp. AFA77.

FOCUS ON PLUTO, Virginia Elenbaas. $4.25p 85pp. AFA74. This book examines Pluto in the houses, signs and aspects. The author relates the material to historic and national events.

FORECASTING WITH NEW, FULL AND QUARTER MOONS, Sophia Mason. $7.00p 170pp. MAS. Mason gives instructions for forecasting with Moon phases and eclipses through all the houses and major aspects.

FORTUNES OF ASTROLOGY, Robert Hurzt Granite. $7.95p ISBN 0-917086-27-9, 128pp. AST81. This book on the Arabic Parts lists over two hundred fortunes and offers three methods of computation plus a fortune-finder. The author's guidelines for multi-level delineation lead to new and personal understanding of these sensitive points.

FOUNDATION OF THE ASTROLOGICAL CHART, Ivy M. Goldstein-Jacobson. $7.50c 325pp. GOJ59. This textbook, designed for home study, shows the way to set up every kind of chart, and presents the basics of astrology. Natal, progressed, horary, solar and lunar returns, ingresses, locality charts, diurnal and "Life Cycle" charts are all discussed with clearly presented mathematics.

FROM HUMANISTIC TO TRANSPERSONAL ASTROLOGY, Dane Rudhyar. $2.50p ISBN 0-916108-05-8, 80pp. SEE75. This book sheds new light on the outer planets of our solar system. Uranus, Neptune and Pluto point the way to the galaxy beyond known limits, guiding us through with their transformative vision.

FROM ONE HOUSE TO ANOTHER, Sophia Mason. $4.00p 67pp. MAS. Mason stresses that to predict the affairs of others through one's own horoscope, the astrologer must understand the houses and their meanings.

FUNDAMENTALS OF BEING AND ASTROLOGY, Istvan S. Meszaros. $9.00p 155pp. ASA81. The author presents an astrological understanding from the metaphysician's point of view. His theme is how astrology can contribute to growth, self-development and greater understanding. This book presents a sound metaphysical foundation to supplement and expand basic understanding on all levels.

FUNDAMENTALS OF NUMBER SIGNIFICANCE, Marc Edmund Jones. $16.50c ISBN 0-87878-015-7, 416pp. AFA. Jones follows the history of horoscopic astrology from its birth through its popularity in the Roman Empire, its decline in medieval Europe, up to the present where modern astrology is asserting itself as a science. Much emphasis is given to the foundational influence of astrology in man's intellectual history, the importance of archaeological discoveries in revealing astrological truths and the inherent mathematical and logical principles embodied in astrology.

GALACTIC DIMENSION OF ASTROLOGY: The Sun is Also a Star, Dane Rudhyar. $7.95p ISBN 0-88231-069-0, 224pp. ASI75. The "challenge of galacticity" to humanistic astrology releases new perspectives when applied to individual horoscopes. Rudhyar expands traditional astrological philosophy by introducing a galactic view of the solar system. He shows how a deeper understanding of Uranus, Neptune and Pluto can be a guide toward experiencing the galactic level of consciousness.

GEODETIC EQUIVALENTS, Sepharial. $2.00p 61pp. AFA. Geodetic equivalents are aids to prediction in mundane astrology, used to measure and adjust the effects of longitude and latitude on the Midheaven and Ascendant. This discussion of the geodetic equivalent also includes proofs of geodetic values, a table of geodetic equivalents of major cities and an analysis of sign rulerships.

GESTALT ASTROLOGY, Tamise Roemer. $10.95p ISBN 0-914918-33-8, 320pp. PAR81. This book offers a new approach to horoscope synthesis and requires no prior astrological knowledge. It shows how to interpret the horoscope as a need gestalt (through the house groupings), a developmental gestalt (linking planets to developmental stages) and a dynamic gestalt (through associate and dissociate aspects and a unique stress scale).

GETTING SPECIFICS OUT OF TRANSITS, Moby Dick. $3.00s 16pp. MOB. Instructions are given on how to predict the future accurately by time cycles. This pamphlet is used for classes in prediction and includes instructions for transit flow charts and the transit dial.

GNOSTIC CIRCLE, Patrizia Norelli-Bachelet. $7.95p 317pp. WEI75. This discussion of the philosophical and gnostic symbolism of both East and West places special emphasis on sacred geometry and numbers. The author writes of the transcendent, the cosmic, the individual and the significance of astrological symbolism to the unfolding of the spirit. The book is well illustrated with color fold-outs and intricate diagrams.

GOD HERSELF: The Feminine Roots of Astrology, Geraldine Thorsten. $14.95c ISBN 0-385-12225-X, 414pp. DOU80.

GODS OF CREATION, Mary Elsnau. $4.00p 50pp. HEA68. A look at the spiritual aspects of astrological symbolism and mythology, the polarity of astrology, the three kings of Persia, Sun, Saturn and Neptune-Mercury.

GOSPEL IN THE STARS or PRIMEVAL ASTRONOMY, Joseph A. Seiss. $12.00s facsimile reprint (1884) 522pp. HEA. This Christian spiritual work deals with the twelve signs in relationship to biblical tradition.

GRAPHIC ASTROLOGY, Ellen McCaffery. $6.75c 316pp. MAC52. This primer presents astrological concepts and the fundamentals of horoscope erection in clear, understandable terms. More than one hundred illustrations and diagrams bring the book to life and make it suitable even for the casual reader.

GUIDEPOSTS TO MUNDANE INTERPRETATION, DeLong. $8.50p AFA.

GUIDE TO HOROSCOPE INTERPRETATION, Marc Edmund Jones. $2.75p ISBN 0-8356-0442-X, THE72; $10.50c ISBN 0-87878-003-3, 208pp. AFA72. Jones describes his system for quickly getting at the heart of a natal chart. He divides all horoscopes into seven easily identified temperament types, and then explains how to interpret them. He applies a similar system to the planets, explaining that these few principles can enable even a novice to recognize the native's dynamic potentials. He illustrates this system with twenty-eight horoscope delineations.

HANDBOOK FOR THE HUMANISTIC ASTROLOGER, Michael Meyer. $5.95p ISBN 0-385-05729-6, 362pp. DOU74. Meyer's comprehensive and lucid exposition of the humanistic approach to astrology, pioneered by Dane Rudhyar, is for the modern astrologer who is more concerned with human growth than with isolated experiences. Meyer correlates planetary cycles with human cycles of existence and gives advice about how people can reach their full potential. The charts of well-known individuals are used for examples.

HANDBOOK OF CHINESE HOROSCOPES, Theodora Lau. $4.95p ISBN 0-06-090752-5, HAR80; $12.95c ISBN 0-06-012521-7, HAR79. The author shows how Chinese astrology, which is based on the lunar calendar, complements Western astrology. She includes chapters on the one hundred forty-four marriage combinations of the twelve signs, and the one hundred forty-four combinations of the lunar signs with the Sun signs. The large volume is engagingly written and instructive to both beginners and more advanced students of astrology.

HANDBOOK OF THE 90 DEGREE DISC: Uranian Astrology, K. H. Ambjornson. $10.00p 218pp. KAM74. This handbook teaches 90 degree disc technique for finding, simply and quickly, all planetary pictures and midpoints in the natal chart, as well as the progressed chart. The book is profusely illustrated and includes problems with answers. It is equally useful in finding midpoint data for the cosmic structural pictures of Ebertin cosmobiology.

HARMONIC ANTHOLOGY, John Addey. $13.95p 148pp. AFA76. This is a collection of important journal articles by Addey on the harmonic viewpoint in astrology. The articles are arranged in historical order and give a unique perspective on the evolution and development of harmonics.

HARMONICS IN ASTROLOGY, John Addey. $15.95p ISBN 85243-344-4, 275pp. FOW76. This is the basic textbook on harmonics in which Addey explains his pioneer work, its general theory and practical applications. The theory of harmonics has important implications for practicing astrologers and provides valuable links with contingent areas of modern scientific research.

HEALING HERBS OF THE ZODIAC, Ada Muir. $1.00p 63pp. WEI59. Muir presents illnesses and healing herbs associated with each of the zodiacal signs.

HERE AND THERE IN ASTROLOGY, Ivy M. Goldstein-Jacobson. $7.50c, 215pp. GOJ61. The first section of this two-part work is a clear presentation of the author's approach to reading various kinds of charts. The second section is devoted to Ms. Goldstein-Jacobsen's original system for drawing up and interpreting event charts.

HERMETIC DREAM, Bob Thibodeau. $4.00p SEK. Horary astrology is applied to dream interpretation.

DAY OF YOUR BIRTH, Bernice Prill Grebner. $6.95p GRE81. This book gives a combined astrological and numerical delineation for your birthday that is not based on the month or the sign.

HIDDEN LAWS OF EARTH, Juliet Brooke Ballard. $4.95p 241pp. ARE. A new look at some seldom-explored subjects from the Edgar Cayce readings. The universal laws affecting incarnations on Earth are discussed with a dynamic view of astrology and its influences. Other topics covered are the Sun and Moon's effect on man and man's effect on the Sun, lunar agriculture, and both cosmic and personal cycles.

HIDDEN MANNA, Patrizia Norelli-Bachelet. $10.00c WEI. This book concerns the zodiac as a symbolic language for initiates of higher wisdom and the sacred geometry of the stars, giving delineations of Revelations, Vedas and Puranas. It shows how occult science, esoteric Christianity and Eastern mythology all transmit the same prophecy.

HINDU BOOK OF ASTROLOGY, Bhakti Seva. $3.50p facsimile reprint (1902) 105pp. HEA. The book discloses yogic knowledge of the stars and planetary forces and how to control them to our advantage.

HINDU HORARY ASTROLOGY, G. Sri Rama Murthi. $4.50p BHA. An English translation of Prasna Tanira.

HISTORY OF ASTROLOGY, Zolar. $7.95c ISBN 0-668-02533-6, 300pp. ARC72. This well-illustrated text covers the history of astrology from the time of the Chaldeans five thousand years ago to our present era.

HOLISTIC ASTROLOGY, Noel Tyl. $15.95c ISBN 0-935620-00-1, 380pp. TAI80. This book centers on psychological analysis within the framework of counseling techniques. The author focuses on external pressures as well as internal development in his presentation of a new understanding of astrology as an integral part of the helping professions.

HOMOSEXUALITY IN THE HOROSCOPE, Karl Guenter Heimsoth. $5.50p AFA.

HORARY ASTROLOGY: The Key to Scientific Prediction, W.J. Simmonite. $5.50p 167pp. AFA50. A nineteenth century horary text, revised in the late nineteenth century by John Story, and revised again by Ernest Grant. It shows how to answer the what, how, and when questions. Data was added by the late Ernest A. Grant.

HORARY ASTROLOGY, Robert DeLuce. $7.50p ISBN 0-88231-035-6, 171pp. ASI. The technique and art of answering specific questions using astrology is explained and further illustrated with thirteen detailed sample charts.

HORARY ASTROLOGY, Geraldine Davis. $4.50p 270pp. SYM/ASA. Davis explains the use of horary astrology in respect to making decisions and choices about travel, relationships, legal matters and business.

HORARY ASTROLOGY, C.C. Zain. $7.25p ISBN 0-87887-343-0, 256pp. CHU30. This method of chart erection is equally applicable to natal astrology, mundane astrology, and stellar diagnosis. Chapter heads include: How to erect a horoscope, the strength and aspects of the planets, the first seven steps to judging any horoscope, houses, etc. Fourteen example charts are included.

HORARY ASTROLOGY AND THE JUDGMENT OF EVENTS, Barbara Watters. $13.50c 220pp. AFA73. The science of horary astrology is outlined and clearly explained with guidelines and definitions. Case histories support the author's study.

HORARY ASTROLOGY, PROBLEM SOLVING, Marc Edmund Jones. $13.50c ISBN 0-87878-004-1, 464pp. AFA. When the original edition was published in 1943, it was the first major work on horary astrology in 300 years. Horary astrology is easy to learn and is the ideal technique for problem solving in practical everyday affairs. A useful primer of symbolism is included in this expanded edition.

HORARY: The Gemini Science, Mae R. Wilson-Ludlam. $4.50p 65pp. MAC73. The twelve case histories used serve as lessons in horary astrology and give insight into the world of the professional astrologer.

HOROSCOPE AS IDENTITY, Noel Tyl. $10.00c 279pp. LLE74. Tyl emphasizes understanding the psychological basis of astrology. He discusses the meaning of Saturn and gives suggestions for its interpretation. Fifty-eight charts illustrate the book.

HOROSCOPE CALCULATION, James A. Eshelman. $10.00p 136pp. AFA. Part I covers the groundwork of astronomy that is pertinent to astrology, with numerous illustrations. Part II contains clear descriptions and examples of horoscope calculations in any astrological system and gives examples of logarithms, motion tables and calculators.

HOROSCOPE DATA SHEETS, $.50 dozen, $1.75 pads of 50 ROS. 8 1/2" x 11". Astrological calculations are simplified with these step-by-step instructions for erecting a chart. A horoscope wheel and calculation blanks are provided.

HOROSCOPE INTERPRETATION OUTLINED, Charles Jayne. $6.00p 53pp. ASB. Jayne explains his preference for first analyzing the natal chart as a whole and then focusing on specific factors. He discusses the major ingredients in a horoscope, the angles and light and their relationships, harmonics, midpoints, Arabic parts, nodes of the Moon and declination parallels.

HOROSCOPE OF MURDER, Doris V. Thompson. $8.50p AFA.

HOROSCOPES: How to Draw and Interpret Them, Brian Innes. $6.95c ISBN 0-668-04553-1, 96pp. ARC. Paintings, sculptures, and poems on the subject of astrology have been reproduced to illustrate the basic steps taken to draw a horoscope. There are one hundred color and black-and-white illustrations.

HOROSCOPES: HERE AND NOW, Robert Carl Jansky. $7.50p 100pp. ASA74. This collection of horoscopes of one hundred contemporary newsmakers can be used by students and teachers alike to illustrate almost all chart features. The charts are accurately and fully drawn, the place, date and time are given and special astrological features are indicated such as T-squares, retrograde rulers and singletons. An index is included.

HOROSCOPES: MUSICIANS AND COMPOSERS, Robert Carl Jansky. $7.50p 100pp. ASA74. One hundred charts of some of the most famous musicians and composers, in both classical and contemporary fields, with an index to birth data for nearly one thousand more. This volume is for those with a special interest in the music field.

HOROSCOPES OF SAINTS & SAGES, Peter L. Holleran. $9.95p ISBN 0-914350-16-1, VUL80. The book is a collection of birth charts of saints and sages throughout the ages, from Jesus Christ to Alan Watts. The author identifies horoscope features which might contribute to the character of a saint or a sage. All birth data sources are listed.

Two Major Astrology Texts by Robert Hand

PLANETS IN TRANSIT
Life Cycles for Living

This is *the* definitive work on transiting planets. Its psychological insight and completeness as a reference book have brought Robert Hand recognition as a leading astrologer. Hand takes a humanistic, multi-leveled approach to transits: the events that may happen, the feelings you may experience, and the possibilities of each transit for growth and awareness.

This book covers complete delineations of all the major transits—conjunction, sextile, square, trine and opposition— that occur between transiting Sun, Moon and all planets to each planet in the natal chart and the Ascendant and Midheaven, as well as complete delineations of each planet transiting each house of the natal chart. These 720 lucid delineations are full of insight for both the professional astrologer and the beginner. 524 pages, paperback, $18.95

PLANETS IN YOUTH
Patterns of Early Developmen

In this book, a major astrologer looks at children and childhood.

As Hand says in his introduction, "...the child as an adult in the process of becoming is the orientation that this book takes."

Not only will parents welcome this book, readers of all ages will use it to understand their own patterns of early development.

The first four chapters discuss parental influences, explain the effects of various planetary energy systems and explore the meanings of all the different factors in a child's chart. There are interpretations of the charts of three children, including Judy Garland and Shirley Temple.

The major part of the book consists of 300-word delineations of horoscope factors. Every planet in every sign and house, as well as in every major aspect, is interpreted in language that emphasizes possibilities. 367 pages, paperback, $12.95.

Available in your local bookstore
Published by Para Research, Whistlestop Mall, Rockport, MA 01966

HOROSCOPES OF THE U.S. STATES AND CITIES, Carolyn Dodson. $10.00p 205pp. DOD75. These computer-prepared charts for the fifty states and their major cities are useful when selecting suitable places to live or predicting future state or city-wide events and trends.

HOROSCOPES OF U.S. PRESIDENTS, Doris Chase Doane. $6.25p 159pp. AFA71. Delineations of horoscopes for all of the United States presidents from Washington to Nixon. These delineations are compared and analyzed to substantiate correlations of astrological factors with vocations, events and disease.

HOROSCOPE SYMBOLS, Robert Hand. $14.95p ISBN 0-914918-16-8, 400pp. PAR80. The author covers such basics as signs, planets, houses and aspects, illuminating their core meanings. In addition, Hand clarifies midpoints, harmonics, the effect of retrograde planets, and analyzes traditional meanings, considers alternatives and uses his twenty years of experience to develop and clarify these symbols. He thoroughly explains astrological symbolism—its history as well as its application for modern astrologers.

HOW TO HANDLE YOUR HUMAN RELATIONS, Lois Haines Sargent. $4.50p 76pp. AFA58. Astrological considerations and modern psychological theories are applied in these practical suggestions for how to improve and harmonize personal relationships and group dynamics, as well as solve conflicts that arise between family members, friends and business partners.

HOW TO HANDLE YOUR T-SQUARE, Tracy Marks. $10.00p ISBN 0-933620-04-7, 208pp. SAG79. This personalized study presents new information on the relatively neglected "T-Square" which the author refers to as"an imbalanced but dynamic configuration." The book includes discussions of opposing signs, opposing houses, the influence of transits and progressions and techniques for analysis and counseling.

HOW TO INTERPRET A BIRTH CHART: A Guide to the Analysis and Synthesis of Astrological Charts, Martin Freeman. $6.95p ISBN 0-85030-249-8, 128pp. WEI81. Freeman explains the basic techniques of natal interpretation for the planets, signs, houses, aspects and nodes.

HOW TO INTERPRET YOUR HOROSCOPE, Judith Leach. $1.95p ISBN 0-06-311054-7, 168pp. HAR78. This introductory guide covers the basics and gives keyword interpretations of the planets in each of the houses and signs, the Ascendant, rulers and more. The author discusses how to balance astrological factors to get an accurate chart reading.

HOW TO JUDGE A NATIVITY, Alan Leo. $6.95p ISBN 0-89281-177-3, 358pp. INT/WEI69. Leo treats the nativity from an entirely practical level, explaining how to assess the occupations and activities of life in great detail, from health, wealth, and the home to philosophy and travel. Comprehensive analysis of the individual houses as they relate to chart interpretation, as well as planetary positions and aspects.

HOW TO LEARN ASTROLOGY, Marc Edmund Jones. $2.95p ISBN 0-394-73342-8, 190pp. SHA41; $10.50c ISBN 0-87878-002-5, 208pp. AFA. Complete, simplified instructions are given for constructing and reading a horoscope. When first published in 1941 the book's method was revolutionary, but today it is the standard for teaching astrology. The beginner starts interpreting the horoscope before learning to recognize the planets, signs and houses, or memorizing a single symbol. The horoscopic elements are thoroughly demonstrated.

HOW TO LIVE WITH THE STARS, Marc Edmund Jones. $3.45p ISBN 0-8356-0473-X; $8.95c ISBN 0-8356-0476-4, 160pp. THE76. This study of transits and their impact on the horoscope begins by tracing and interpreting the cycles of the planets. Knowledge of the use of an ephemeris and a basic understanding of horoscopes is necessary. Jones uses Watergate and Richard Nixon to illustrate his exposition.

HOW TO PREPARE AND PASS AN ASTROLOGER'S CERTIFICATE EXAM, Doris Chase Doane. $5.00p 56pp. AFA73. This little book is designed to give the astrologer confidence about taking astrological examinations.

HOW TO READ COSMODYNES, Doris Chase Doane, $4.95p 49pp. AFA74. This is a detailed, graphically illustrated explanation of how to use and mathematically compute "stellar dynamics." Cosmodynes aid in determining energy levels by "Judging the relative power, harmony and discord of the four basic factors in the natal and progressed chart—planets, signs, houses and aspects—by employing astrodynes, harmodynes, and discordynes."

HOW TO READ THE EPHEMERIS, Jeff Mayo. $3.50p ISBN 85243-057-4, 308pp. FOW66. This attractive book gives careful explanations of all the data to be found in an ephemeris and table of houses, together with instructions for their use. Both beginners and more advanced students can benefit from it.

HOW TO SEDUCE ANY MAN IN THE ZODIAC, Robin MacNaughton. $2.95p ISBN 0-553-01226-6, 96pp. BAN80. Based on the twelve Sun signs, this book describes the likes and dislikes of men.

HOW TO SET UP A BIRTH CHART, John Filbey. $7.00p ISBN 0-85030-246-3, 128pp. AQU81. This complete guide to the practical techniques of casting a horoscope explains the astronomical basis, time changes, house systems, how to use reference material, calculations and natal charting.

HOW TO USE THE CELL SALTS, Robert Carl Jansky. $2.50p 29pp. ASA77. A practical guide to choosing and using the proper biochemic cell salts in preventive medicine, based upon the natal chart (excerpted from MODERN MEDICAL ASTROLOGY).

IMPORTANCE OF MERCURY IN THE HOROSCOPE, Frances Sakoian and Louis Acker. $2.00p 41pp. NES70. Beginning with a broad look at Mercury, this phamphlet goes on to analyze Mercury in the signs, in retrograde positions and in each of the houses.

IMPROVED PERPETUAL PLANETARY HOUR BOOK, Llewellyn George. $5.00p ISBN 0-87542-270-5, 217pp. LLE75. This book gives the correct planetary rulership and astrological significance, so valuable in electional astrology, for every hour of every day.

INFINITE HORIZONS: A Psychic Experience, Michael J. Brady. $5.95p ISBN 0-89865-042-9, DON. Brady focuses on the question of humanity's past, present and future and discusses many pressing questions concerning its existence and future. He delves into the search for the soul, karmic astrology and reincarnation, reunited lovers and human destiny. He includes the natal charts of some of his famous clients.

INFLUENCE OF PLUTO ON LOVE LIFE, Reinhold Ebertin. $3.50p 29pp. HBV70. Ebertin has investigated the influence of Pluto on human life for many years. He discusses Pluto's influence and its aspects to other constellations and planets. Many illustrative charts are included.

INFLUENCE OF THE HOUSES: ASTRO-KINETICS Vol I, Edward W. Whitman. $8.00c ISBN 85243-168-6, 200pp. FOW70. This first in a series of three books dealing with applied astrology analyzes and explains the influence of each individual house of the zodiac to clarify just how to set about the delineation of a horoscope.

INFLUENCE OF THE PLANET PLUTO, Elbert Benjamine. $1.50p ISBN 0-933646-16-X, 32pp. ARI81. This monthly ephemeris of Pluto from 1840 to 1990 also contains the results of an investigation of seven thousand birth charts of natal and progressed positions of Pluto by the Brotherhood of Light Research Department.

INFLUENCE OF THE PLANETS: ASTRO-KINETICS Vol II, Edward W. Whitman. $8.00c ISBN 85243-170-8, 252pp. FOW70. This second book in the series explains in a scientific yet lucid way, how each of the signs of the zodiac has a definite planetary ruler and how each planet is more favorably placed in certain signs than in others.

INFLUENCE OF THE STARS, Rosa Baughan. $5.00s facsimile reprint (1904) 272pp. HEA. The three sections of this book cover astrology, chiromancy and physiognomy.

IN OTHER WOMEN'S HOUSES, Barbara Donchess. $3.50p ISBN 0-914350-27-7, 80pp. VUL78. This is the companion piece to HOW TO COPE WITH HIS HOROSCOPE, written for men. The author draws on her clinical experience to delineate the planets in the houses of the woman's natal chart. She offers a humorous approach to human relationships.

IN SEARCH OF A FULFILLING CAREER, Joanne Wickenburg. $5.50p 117pp. SEA77. An astrological guide for understanding and fulfilling vocational needs. All signs, houses and planets are discussed in relation to vocational concerns. Individual interpretations are furnished for signs and houses, their ruling planets and occupant planets.

INSTANTANEOUS HOROSCOPE DELINEATOR, Dorothy Hughes. $2.95 HUG. This shows how to find the approximate rising sign and house cusps for any time, any day of the year and any place in the world without mathematics.

INTERCEPTED SIGNS: Environment vs Destiny, Joanne Wickenburg. $5.95p 101pp. SEA. This in-depth interpretation of each sign when intercepted discusses the ruling planets as well as occupying intercepted signs and offers suggestions for the constructive use of their energies. Duplicated signs are also covered in relation to the interceptions to give a more total picture of how the entire chart is affected when intercepted signs are present.

INTERFACE: PLANETARY NODES, Michael and Margaret Erlewine and David Wilson. $5.00p 25pp. AFA76. Designed to be used with the heliocentric coordinate system, these are tables of the planetary nodes' interface points from 1700 to 2001. Instructions are included.

INTERPRETATION: Jungian Symbolism and Astrology, Karen Hamaker-Zondag. ISBN 0-87728-523-3, WEI. The author combines the concepts of Jungian psychology and the symbology of the astrological chart. She works with the crosses and the elements in an unusual manner. This book will interest both the student and professional.

INTERPRETATION: PLANETARY & AGE CYCLES, Angela Louise Gallo. $10.00p 183pp. CHM78. Gallo charts the rise and fall of each transiting planet through the zodiac cycle. She interprets every planet in each quarter with the positive and negative aspects in every house.

INTERPRETATING SOLAR RETURNS, James A. Eshelman. $8.50p 167pp. ASA79. This definitive work on solar returns gives interpretations of planetary meanings with instructive examples.

INTERPRETING THE ASPECTS, Robert Carl Jansky. $8.00p 70pp. ASA78. This is an in-depth study of the principles behind aspect interpretation and the various geometric configurations such as the T-Square, Grand Trine, Yod and Kite. Contemporary midpoint theory is the perspective through which the strengths and weaknesses of the aspects are presented.

INTERPRETING THE ECLIPSES, Robert Carl Jansky. $6.00p 60pp. AST77. This meticulous investigation is a practical guide to the importance and use of the solar eclipse in delineation, rectification, and yearly forecasting. Many case studies are included.

INTERPRETING THE HOUSES, Helen Paul and Bridget Mary O'Toole. $8.00p 96pp. ASA76. There is a considerable amount of information available on the symbolic interpretation of the houses, which the authors have compiled in a single reference book. In addition to the detailed house descriptions, there are chapters on how to handle intercepted signs, sign polarities and a technique for "rotating the chart."

INTERPRETING YOUR SUN-ASCENDANT, Joan McEvers. $9.00p 205pp. ASA80. One hundred forty-four delineations of Sun-Ascendant combinations are further defined by the decanate of the Sun and Ascendant. An example chart illustrates every combination and all chart data and source information are given. A book for initiates and more advanced astrologers.

INTERPRET YOUR CHART, Mae R. Wilson-Ludlam. $6.00p 157pp. MAC73. This comprehensive easy-to-follow method gives keyword interpretations for all twelve sets of cusps, one hundred forty-four Sun-Moon combinations, and directions for "phrasing" the planets and aspects. Example charts are provided. Applying and separating aspects are also explained, as well as intercepted planets, progressions, transits, decans, Moon's nodes, the dark moon Lilith, the Part of Fortune and event astrology. Questions and answers are included.

INTERPRET YOUR RAYS, Mae R. Wilson-Ludlam. AFA81. Publication is forthcoming.

INTERVIEWING AND COUNSELING TECHNIQUES FOR ASTROLOGERS, Reverend Marvin Layman. $4.00p 42pp. ASB74. The author shares his extensive experience in pastoral counseling in his book on the psychology of the astrological interview. He documents his presentation with a number of case studies and illustrates the book with charts.

INTRODUCTION TO LOCALITY ASTROLOGY, Charles Jayne. $5.00p ASB. The accompanying diagrams and tables facilitate the teaching of locality astrology. Jayne also discusses the Johndro chart.

LECTURES ON MEDICAL ASTROLOGY, William Davidson. $2.50p ASB.

IT IS ALL RIGHT, Isabel M. Hickey. $7.50c 141pp. HIC. Hickey's book deals with an understanding of the cosmic laws and relates many experiences that prove those laws. She discusses death, how to tell children about God, the mating games, alcoholism, meditation and guidance.

JEANE DIXON'S ASTROLOGICAL COOKBOOK, Jeane Dixon. $6.95c ISBN 03091-2, 250pp. WIM76. This cookbook explains how to select foods astrologically to harmonize with the body chemistry and temperament of persons born in each of the twelve signs.

JESUS WAS A LEO, Frank Jakubowsky. $6.95c ISBN 0-932588-01-8, 151pp. JAK79. This controversial book claims to scientifically prove the time of Jesus Christ's birth. The position of the planets at his birth creates a pattern identical to the pattern of his parables. It answers scientific and religious objections to astrology by offering a new scientific theory on how astrology works on a biological and chemical level.

JOHNDRO'S THEORY OF PLANETARY RULERSHIPS, Al Morrison. $2.00p 14pp. AFA72. A collection of selected notes taken by Morrison during W. Kenneth Brown's lecture series on the Johndro material.

JUDAH'S SCEPTRE AND JOSEPH'S BIRTHRIGHT, Rev. J.H. Allen. $8.50 facsimile reprint (1917) 448pp. HEA. The story of the twelve sons of Jacob and their future, as taken from the Bible.

JUPITER: The Preserver, Alan Leo. $2.50p 88pp. WEI73. A reprint of lectures given in 1916. Leo compares Jupiter and Saturn, the separative structuring of Saturn, the unfolding of Jupiter. He discusses Jupiter symbolism as it relates to oriental philosophy, esoteric astrology and personal expression. A scholarly work on the planet.

JUPITER THROUGH THE STARS, Frederic van Norstrand. $4.25p 40pp. CLA80. The author gives a thorough background on the history and symbolism of Jupiter and looks at Jupiter in each of the twelve signs. Tables from 1900 to 2000 are included.

KARMIC ASTROLOGY, Vol 1: The Moon's Nodes and Reincarnation, Martin Schulman. $3.95p ISBN 0-87728-288-9, 133pp. WEI75. Many astrologers believe that the nodes of the Moon represent karmic influences manifesting in the present life. Schulman examines the nodes in each of the signs and houses and clarifies many concepts. There are chapters on aspects to the nodes, sample delineations and an appendix giving nodal positions for 1850 to 2000 A.D.

KARMIC ASTROLOGY, Vol 2: Retrogrades and Reincarnation, Martin Schulman. $4.95p ISBN 0-87728-345-1, 204pp. WEI77. Schulman's book represents a major shift in interpretation of retrogradation. His delineations of retrograde planets in the signs and houses assign neither positive nor negative traits. They illustrate his concept of reincarnation and karma, showing how individuals may use their energy in unproductive ways and how each person needs to mature.

KARMIC ASTROLOGY, Vol 3: Joy and the Part of Fortune, Martin Schulman. $4.95p ISBN 0-87728-346-X, 115pp. WEI78. The author explains the placement of the Part of Fortune in the twelve signs and houses, with example charts and delineations of notable nativities. Throughout, the laws of karma are related to this mysterious and vital point in the horoscope.

KARMIC ASTROLOGY, Vol 4: The Karma of Now, Martin Schulman. $4.95p ISBN 0-87728-416-4, 125pp. WEI79. In this final volume of his series on karma, Schulman takes the planets through the signs showing how to use the planetary energies to avoid limitations from the past and unrealistic expectations for the future.

KARMIC RELATIONSHIPS, Martin Schulman. $6.95p ISBN 0-87728-508-X, 144pp. WEI81. The author examines the astrology of karmic relationships. He discusses how aspects influence men and women differently, why relationships develop on many levels and the unconscious workings of the anima-animus in relationships.

KEY CYCLE, Wynn. $3.00p 56pp. AFA. This is an original approach for interpreting daily, weekly and monthly influences in the natal chart. Relevant details are presented along with many sample interpretations. It also includes a table of instant timing of future vibrations.

KEY FACTOR TO MOTIVATION, Olson and Hanratty. $6.95p AFA.

KEY TO INTER-RELATIONS, Clara M. Darr. $3.25p 25pp. DAR61. The author's guidelines to important factors in chart comparison cite aspects to the nodes, Fortuna or the Part of Fortuna, the Ascendant and the Midheaven. Karmic points of contact are also noted.

KEY TO ASTROLOGY, Raphael. $2.50s facsimile reprint 108pp. HEA. Containing a complete system of genethliacal astrology. Corrected and revised.

KEY TO YOUR OWN NATIVITY, Alan Leo. $6.95p ISBN 0-89281-179-X, 328pp. INT/WEI69. Leo's complete and comprehensive analysis of all the elements of the horoscope prepares the beginning student by giving full descriptions of every position in the nativity. He shows where to find indications in the horoscope related to topics such as finance, travel, health, marriage, legacies, partnership, profession, and occultism.

KEYWORD SYSTEM, $.50p 16pp. ROS. This practical simplified method of horoscope interpretation uses keywords for each of the signs, planets, houses, and aspects. The system is based on the teachings of Max Heindel.

KNOW YOUR ASCENDANT, Chauncey D. King. $3.00p 78pp. AFA. King's system of elimination is presented by first finding the right sign on the Ascendant and then following it with a good method of verifying Ascendant choice. The system is clearly illustrated, and the use of the term "Epoch Day" is easily learned through examples.

KNOW YOUR NUMBER, Charles Misegades. $5.50p ISBN 0-87516-388-2, 169pp. DEV. This book combines astrology, numerology, and Cabala to pinpoint the troubled areas of our globe. The geographical zodiac makes it possible to see the nature of Uranus, Neptune, Saturn and Pluto transits and how individuals and governments may deal with them.

LABOURS OF HERCULES, Alice Bailey. $3.25p 111pp. LUC74. This is the story of Hercules passing through the twelve Sun signs of the zodiac. In each sign he expressed its characteristics and achieved some fresh knowledge of himself. Through that knowledge he demonstrated the power of the sign and acquired the gifts which the sign conferred. In each of the signs he surmounted his natural tendencies, controlling and governing his destiny, and demonstrated the fact that the stars incline, but do not control.

LADDER OF THE PLANETS, Frances Sakoian and Louis Acker. $2.50p 27pp. NES74. This is a short exposition of zodiacal rulerships and exaltations which includes material on Uranus, Pluto and Neptune.

LADY, I HAVE YOUR NUMBER, Douglas H. Miller. $3.50p 44pp. AFA72. This manual gives a formula for using the accompanying tables and additional material for computing individual astrological birth control.

LECTURES ON MEDICAL ASTROLOGY, William Davidson. $12.50p 142pp. ASB73. These eight lectures, given by the author, are accompanied by a six-page contents section containing highlights for every page in the book. Useful as a quick reference source.

LIFE OF KING CHARLES, John Gadbury. $4.75p 128pp. DAR74. This 1659 classic is valuable material for historical research. Life's trials, tribulations and joys are astrologically analyzed.

LIFE SIGNS, AN ASTROLOGICAL CASEBOOK, Mary Jones and Dan Fry. $4.95p ISBN 0-915442-77-9, 120pp. DON79. According to Dan Fry, the stars influence, they do not dictate. The validity of astrology, however, is in the highly individual charts which indicate one's natural abilities and inclinations. Life Signs tells the stories of twenty-one such individuals who have used or ignored the advice of this astrologer.

LILITH INSIGHT, Mae R. Wilson-Ludlam. $6.50p 124pp. MAC. The author discusses Lilith in the signs, houses, critical degrees, the positive purpose of Lilith, Lilith in the horary chart and the forty-day spiritual cycle. The author offers keywords for Lilith and includes a notebook, example charts and illustrations.

LIVELY CIRCLE, Barbara Koval. $9.95p ISBN 0-917086-27-9, 128pp. AST81. The validity of astrology is addressed in the context of scientific skepticism and twentieth-century human needs. In correcting the misconceptions that surround the ancient art of astrology, the author demonstrates how astrological symbolism relates to such stubborn questions as fate and free will, environment and heredity, fact and theory and the validity of prediction.

LIVES YOU LIVE AS REVEALED IN THE HEAVENS, Ted George. $12.00c ISBN 0-932782-00-0, 196pp. ART. This thorough guide to reading the chart from a karmic standpoint contains chapters on previous lives in the twelfth house, first house, fourth house, tenth house, fifth house and the advancement of the soul in the nineth house. It also includes information and delineations of the two unknown planets, Vulcan and Persephone.

THE LOST KEY TO PREDICTION: The Arabic Parts in Astrology, Robert E. Zoller. $8.95p ISBN 0-89281-013-0, 256pp. INT/WEI80. Zoller unravels the ancient doctrine of the Arabic parts by exploring the interrelationship of macrocosm and microcosm through numbers. He applies the esoteric nature of numbers to reveal the essence of karma or fate in astrology. He includes his translation of an important Latin text on the the parts and a discussion of the practical use of the parts in natal, mundane and horary astrology.

LOVE, SEX AND ASTROLOGY, Teri King. $2.95p ISBN 0-06-464000-0, 243pp. HAR73. A basic character analysis is given for each sign. Using Sun signs as a guide, the author explains compatibility with other Sun signs illustrated by two tables of attractions for men and women. A basic character analysis is also given for each sign.

LOVE SIGNS, Linda Goodman. $15.00c ISBN 0-06-011550-5, 1186pp. HAR78. Using the Sun signs to determine compatibility, Linda Goodman explores the chances for success and happiness of relationships. Breaking down the male and female components for each sign, she shows how both men and women will most likely relate to either sex of all the other signs.

LUNAR ASTROLOGY, Alexandre Volguine. $8.95c ISBN 0-88231-004-6, 136pp. ASI74. The astrology of antiquity recognized a lunar zodiac and lunar houses. Volguine believes the role of the Moon in astrology is too small. He discusses the twenty-eight lunar mansions and lunar houses, giving modern examples to support the description according to the Hindu asterisms, the Manazils of the Arabs, the Chinese Siu and the Hebraic esoteric tradition, Kabala.

LUNAR EFFECT: Biological Tides and Human Emotions, Arnold L. Lieber. $7.95p AFA. This book scientifically investigates the influence of the Moon on mankind. Dr. Lieber uses case studies to illustrate that violent behavior such as murder, aggravated assault, suicide, psychiatric emergencies and fatal auto accidents increase dramatically at the time of certain Moon phases.

LUNAR NODES, Mohan Koparkar. $4.95p ISBN 0-918922-04-6, 90pp. MOH77. This comprehensive book of lunar nodes begins with a basic discussion of the nodes and then introduces the concepts of karmic controls in life and controlling aspects. Other chapters delineate the nodes through the signs and houses, aspects of nodes to natal and progressed planets, transiting nodes and their effects, nodes in synastry, transiting planets to the nodal axis and more.

LUNATION CYCLE: A Key to the Understanding of Personality, Dane Rudhyar. $3.95p ISBN 0-394-73020-8, 138pp. SHA71. Rudhyar shows how the lunation cycle, the cycle relationship of the Moon to the Sun, helps to explain human behavior.

LUNATIONS AND PREDICTIONS, Sophia Mason and Mary Lou Shephard. $4.00p 68pp. MAS76. The authors show how full and new moon lunations can be used in making astrological predictions and discuss lunations in the houses.

LURE OF THE HEAVENS: A HISTORY OF ASTROLOGY, Donald Papon. $7.95p ISBN 0-87728-502-0, 320pp. WEI80. This authoritative work traces the origins and development of astrology through thousands of years and many civilizations.

MAN AND HIS WORLD, Bruno and Louise Huber. $5.95p ISBN 0-87728-413-X, 117pp. WEI78. These authors have a message for both the beginning student of astrology as well as those especially interested in the psychological approach to the ancient science. The Hubers discuss the psychological significance of the horoscope and give special emphasis to the houses and quadrants of the chart as these factors symbolize the various human functions of life.

MAN AND THE ZODIAC, David Anrias. $5.95p ISBN 0-87728-014-2, 224pp. WEI70. This astrological study provides methods of synchronizing the planets, houses and their mutual aspects and includes solid definitions of the signs and their decanates. Signs are discussed in relation to the conscious, unconscious and superconscious.

MAN IN THE UNIVERSE, Reinhold Ebertin. $7.00p 104pp. HBV73. Ebertin's introductory presentation of cosmobiology includes the working methods of casting a natal chart, an evaluation of the elements, determination of midpoints, interpretation and other supplementary techniques.

MAPS OF CONSCIOUSNESS, Ralph Metzner. $4.95p ISBN 0-02-077400-1, 160pp. MAM74. These maps are the traditional occult tools of the I Ching, Tarot, tantra, astrology, actualism and alchemy. Each topic is extensively discussed with an accompanying bibliography and many references.

MARK EDMUND JONES 500, Marc Edmund Jones. $6.95p ISBN 0-88231-04-2, 190pp. ASI. For many years, students of the Sabian Assembly asked Marc Edmund Jones to spontaneously interpret charts without prior study. In this way, he could analyze each step without skipping details a beginner would need but which might be passed over by the expert. Five hundred of these horoscope sessions have been taped and transcribed to date. Ten sessions are included in each of these volumes.

MARS, THE WAR LORD, Alan Leo. $2.50p 99pp. WEI73. These are reprints from Leo's 1915 lectures to the Astrological Society, in which he discusses Mars and its significant influence in the horoscopes of ten famous people. Mars is discussed with respect to force, assertiveness, the struggle for consciousness, the material world, youth, ambition, maturity and a spiritual consciousness in this changing world.

MASTER GUIDE TO PREPARING YOUR NATAL HOROSCOPE, King Keyes. $3.45p ISBN 013-560003-0; $7.95c ISBN 013-559930-X, 214pp. PRE74. Keyes' step-by-step guidebook explains the use of basic astrological tools including an ephemeris and table of houses. The test questions are graphically answered with illustrations and explanations are given for the necessary mathematical calculations in chart erection.

MATHEMATICAL ASTROLOGY, Mohan Koparkar. $4.25p 105pp. AFA74. Koparkar gives interpretive presentations of techniques and includes the corresponding diagrams and charts. He covers planetary power, periods and transits, chart magnification, marriage compatibility and the fixed stars.

MECHANICS OF TABLES OF HOUSES, J. Allen Jones. $6.00p ISBN 0-912368-07-1, 65pp. GOL74. Jones offers diagrams and explanations of the mathematics necessary for several house divisions including the Placidus, Regiomontanus and Campanus systems. FOR ABOVE THE ARTIC CIRCLE is also included with many examples and diagrams of the necessary mathematical procedures for calculating Placidian cusps.

MEDICAL ASTROLOGY, Boris Paque. $16.50c ISBN 0-88231-051-8, ASI80. A systematic and in-depth approach to medical astrology.

MEDICAL ASTROLOGY, Heinrich Daath. $2.00p 108pp. HEA. Illustrated.

MEDITATIONS ON THE SIGNS OF THE ZODIAC, John Jocelyn. $5.95p ISBN 0-06-066092-9, 288pp. HAR80. This old standard contains meditations on each of the twelve signs of the zodiac. Jocelyn uses traditional astrological symbolism but also envisions a Christ-centered zodiac in which each of the signs relate to some facet of the New Testament. Continuing in this approach, the author relates the signs to a developing Christ-consciousness within and gives helpful suggestions to the spiritual seeker.

MELODY OF LIFE AND LOVE, Ivy M. Goldstein-Jacobson. $5.50c 89pp. GOJ76. A collection of verses that includes the planets, stressing Mercury's importance. A few of these appear in the Introduction of ASTROLOGICAL ESSAYS.

MERCURY METHOD OF CHART COMPARISON, Lois M. Rodden. $9.50c 214pp. AFA73. The Mercury method is a chart comparison technique in which the aspects of Mercury are drawn in one chart to the planets in another chart, to give a perspective on the relationship.

MESSAGE OF THE STARS, Max Heindel and Augusta Foss Heindel. $6.00p; $9.00c 728pp. ROS73. The Heindels, active in astrology and Rosicrucianism early in this century, discuss the fundamentals of astrological interpretation, the keyword system of chart analysis. The meanings of the planets, signs and the thirty-six example charts suggest methods for making progressions and predictions. The authors explain their system of medical diagnosis, based on their own practical experience.

METAPHYSICAL ASTROLOGY, John Hazelrigg. $2.00p facsimile reprint (1900) 71pp. HEA. The author discusses the rationale of astrology, inductive astrology, symbolism, eclipses and nature's analogies.

MIDPOINT INTERPRETATION SIMPLIFIED, Savalan. $10.00p AFA.

MIDPOINT LOVE SIMPLIFIED, Savalan. $10.00p AFA.

MIDPOINT SYNASTRY SIMPLIFIED, Savalan. $10.00p AFA.

MINERVA OR PLUTO: The Choice is Yours, Isabel M. Hickey. $4.95p 83pp. HIC74. Hickey discusses the nature and meaning of Pluto and its twin Charon, which she calls Minerva. She agrees that Pluto is the highest or lowest energy we can use or abuse. Meanings are defined for Pluto in the signs and houses, in aspect and in transit. Also included are a number of letters to the author with her responses and accompaning charts.

MINOR ASPECTS, Frances Sakoian and Louis Acker. $2.75p 60pp. NES78. The minor aspects are defined and delineated.

MINOR ASPECTS BETWEEN THE NATAL PLANETS, Emma Donath. $9.00p 224pp. EDO/AFA81. This planet-by-planet discussion of the minor aspects covers the vigintile, semi-sextile, novile, semi-square, quintile, and sesquiquadrate. Aimed at beginning and professional astrologers.

MISSING MOON, Noel Tyl. $4.95p ISBN 0-87542-797-9, 165pp. LLE79. Tyl blends fiction, humor and imagination with astrological practices. The hero-astrologer, Michael Mercury, in this collection of short stories goes through a trial by exaggeration and misadventure. Anecdotally, Tyl takes his hero through the comedy and humor of the horoscope, hyperbolically challenging and reinforcing the knowledge of practical astrology.

MODERN INTRODUCTION TO ASTROLOGY, Henry Weingarten. $1.95p ISBN 0-88231-014-3, 83pp. ASI. This unique book explores astrology from a modern viewpoint. It gives scientific evidence and shows how astrology may be applied to many fields including business, education, medicine, psychology and politics.

MODERN MEDICAL ASTROLOGY, Robert Carl Jansky. $8.00p ASA74. This volume examines the relationships between planets, signs, parts of the body and their correct function. Cell salts are related to the signs and vitamins and minerals to the planets. The case studies illustrate the author's discussion of such topics as alcoholism, asthma, birth control, diabetes and violence. The author uses both classical and modern research techniques for diagnosis.

MODERN TRANSITS, Lois M. Rodden. $8.95p AFA. This textbook includes the major cycles of transits and illustrates how they modify, shape, color and add dimension and timing to major progressed aspects.

MOON MANSIONS, Mohan Koparkar. $4.50p ISBN 0-918922-01-1, 92pp. MOH74. An idea of dividing the zodiac into twenty-seven equal parts, instead of the usual twelve signs, is used here to get a wider spectrum of chart analyses. The author delineates each of ten planets and the Ascendant in each of the twenty-seven lunar mansions. Also included is an astronomical illustration of each of the mansions.

MOON SIGNS, Sybil Leek. $1.95p BER.

MOON'S NODES AND THEIR INFLUENCE ON NATAL ASTROLOGY, G. White. $1.95p 74pp. WEI. In this 1927 study, White evaluates the meaning of the nodes and how their position can affect physical stature as well as success or fame. He also covers the relationships of the nodes to the signs and houses, the Sun and Moon, and eclipses.

MORE MYSTERIES OF ASTROLOGY, Mary Elsnau. $4.00p HEA. Illustrated, lithographed, typewritten format.

MORINUS SYSTEM OF INTERPRETATION, Morin de Villefrance. $5.00p 109pp. AFA74. Richard Baldwin has translated Morin's formidable early seventeenth century work which forms a basis for contemporary astrological interpretation. Morin attempted to take the superstition out of medieval astrology.

MUNDANE ASTROLOGY, C.C. Zain. $8.00p ISBN 0-87887-350-3, 320pp. CHU39. The author asserts that when world leaders are aware of astrological influences and planetary positions, they can better plan national and international policy under astrological advisement. Includes the doctrine of mundane astrology, the cycles and major conjunctions of the planets and precise predicting of eclipses.

MUNDANE PERSPECTIVES IN ASTROLOGY, Marc Edmund Jones. $16.50c ISBN 0-87878-014-9, 463pp. AFA75. In this sequel to the Scope of Astrological Prediction, Jones demonstrates the influence of the Arabian parts and the geocentric nodes using his own chart as an example. Eight decades of American history are interpreted by illustrating the influence of the transits and progressions of American presidents on national events during their respective terms in the White House.

MYSTERIES OF ASTROLOGY AND THE WONDERS OF MAGIC, Dr. C.W. Roback. $6.00s facsimile reprint (1854) 236pp. HEA. The author explores the history, rise and progress of astrology and necromancy. Also given are directions and suggestions relative to the casting of nativities and predictions by geomancy, chiromancy and physiognomy. The book is interspersed with many diagrams, formulae and divinations.

MY WORLD OF ASTROLOGY, Sydney Omarr. $5.00p ISBN 0-87980-103-4, 378pp. WIL65. Sydney Omarr shares his understanding of how astrology influences the lives of men and women. General instructions are given for casting and interpreting birth charts and interpreting the signs, planets, cusps and transits. The author gives a personal view of how astrology influences his life.

NADI SYSTEM OF RECTIFICATION, Marc Penfield. $6.60p ISBN 0-914350-22-6, 29pp. VUL77. The Nadi system is a Hindu method of rectifying the actual time of birth for a horoscope which Penfield has personally tested on two thousand charts. He sumarizes the steps to be followed in the Nadi system, gives examples of the system in operation and provides a series of tables.

NATAL ASTROLOGY: DELINEATING THE HOROSCOPE, C.C. Zain. $7.50p ISBN 0-87887-341-4, 256pp. CHU73. Zain explains how to choose the most supportive environmental conditions to develop natural talents. He analyzes the thirty-six decants and discusses traits of the signs and planets.

NATAL ASTROLOGY: PROGRESSING THE HOROSCOPE, C.C. Zain. $7.00p ISBN 0-87887-342-2, 256pp. CHU73. In Zain's explanation of the Hermetic system of progressions, he reviews major and minor progressions of the Sun and angles, the Moon and planets. Transits, revolutions, cycles and rectifying the horoscope are also included.

NATAL CHARTING: How to Master the Techniques of Birth Chart Construction, John Filbey. $8.95p ISBN 0-85030-246-3, 192pp. WEI81. This is a complete guide to the practical techniques of casting a horoscope and includes the astronomical basis, time changes, house systems, how to use reference material, calculations and natal charting.

NATURAL BIRTH CONTROL BOOK, Rosenblum. $4.95p. ISBN 0-916726-01-0, 156pp. AQR77. A tested method developed by Dr. Jonas and others in Czechoslovakia is described. Evidence of its success in America is included along with scientific research. Full instructions and computerized charts are provided so that no calculations are required.

NEPTUNE EFFECT, Patricia Morimando. $3.95p ISBN 0-87728-487-3, 74pp. WEI79. This book discusses the varying manifestations of Neptunian energy and attitudes and shows how to benefit from understanding the presence and function of this elusive planet in the natal chart.

NEPTUNE: HOW TO SWIM THROUGH COSMIC WATERS, Tracy Marks. $2.50p 19pp. SAG. Marks presents her understanding of the psychological experience of Neptune, whether natally or by transit, and how it can be channeled. She focuses its often confusing and depleting energy upon levels of consciousness, attunement to inner guidance, coping with confusion and ambiguity, using fantasy and imagery and the nature of giving and spirituality.

NEPTUNE IN TRANSIT, Clara M. Darr. $3.75p 43pp. DAR75. This work takes Neptune through the houses and gives the five major aspects.

NEW AGE ASTROLOGER: Vol 1, John Soric. $9.95c 324pp. STA76. This basic textbook for the beginning student analyses the planets through the rising signs, aspects, signs and houses. Chart construction is also discussed.

NEW AGE CAREER CYCLES: A Planetary Guide to the Patterns of Opportunity, John Townley. $7.95p ISBN 0-89281-006-8, 192pp. INT/WEI. The key provided here shows how to benefit from planetary rhythms instead of being controlled by them. It unfolds planetary rhythms, demonstrating business and career matters. By using graphs and charts provided, you will determine your peak success cycles and how to make the most of them.

NEW CONCEPTION OF SIGN RULERSHIP, L. Edward Johndro. $2.00p 30pp. AFA71. This companion piece to ASTROLOGICAL DICTIONARY provides an approach for examining the relationship of the individual to his environment and society.

NEW DIMENSION IN ASTROLOGY, Charles Jayne. $3.00p 31pp. ASB75. Eclipses, occultations, cazimis and other alignments of planets to the Sun are discussed as well as conjunctions and oppositions without latitude. Tables give eclipses and cazimis for eighty-four years and occultations for recent years.

NEW FOUNDATIONS FOR ASTROLOGY, David and Gina Cochrane. $5.00p ISBN 0-88231-07-4, 96pp. ASI79. This work on degree analysis correlates the Hindu system of divisional charts with modern harmonic degree analysis. Rather than giving fixed and fatalistic interpretations, the authors analyze each degree by energy and function and provide guides to interpretations whereby the student can discover any degree's meaning.

NEW MANSIONS FOR NEW MEN, Dane Rudhyar. $6.95p ISBN 0-89793-002-9, 273pp. HUN78. Rudhyar's poetic work treats the science of astrology as a system of symbols. This volume on psycho-spiritual astrology is, as the author says, for everyone who wishes to go deeper into the substratum and the meaning of human experience in terms of consciousness and understanding.

NODE BOOK, Zipporah P. Dobyns. $4.00p TIA73. Tables of longitudes of the nodes of the planets from a geocentric point of view from 1971-1974 are given, with a table of equivalent years applicable to any year. The Moon's nodes in the six zodiacal polarities with illustrative examples are included.

NODES IN TRANSIT, Clara M. Darr. $3.75p 54pp. DAR76. The author examines the meaning of the north and south nodes transiting each of the natal planets and their own natal positions.

NORTH AND SOUTH NODES: The Guideposts of the Spirit, Ted George. $4.95p ISBN 0-932782-02-7, 100pp. ART. This comprehensive interpretation of nodal placements delineates the nodes in the signs and houses, in aspect, conjunct the planets, Vulcan, Persephone, Lilith and conjunct transiting planets.

NOT A SIGN IN THE SKY BUT A LIVING PERSON, Marc Robertson. $3.00p ACN75. Robertson presents the eight personality types and how they relate to the inner-self. This analysis is based on Dane Rudhyar's lunation cycle theory. The author also investigates the progression of the phases of the Moon and the"natural outlets" by house and sign for expressing the personality type.

NOW THAT I'VE CAST IT, WHAT DO I DO WITH IT?, Maxine Taylor. $6.00p 86pp. TAY75. This is designed to increase the beginning student's confidence in being able to interpret charts and not just memorize information. The author uses her basic sentence approach to simplify horoscope interpretation. She discusses planets in the houses and signs, houses, and aspects to the planets and angles.

OCCULT PREPARATIONS FOR A NEW AGE, Dane Rudhyar. $3.25p ISBN 0-8356-0460-8, 275pp. THE75. In this study of man and his universe, Rudhyar affirms not only that the heavens affect humanity, but that humanity affects the heavens. He asserts that to correctly evaluate world conditions today it is necessary to take the long, aeonic view of the evolution of life as a cyclical process. The book includes an overview of Blavatsky's Secret Doctrine and a discussion of the occult brotherhood.

OCCULT SOURCEBOOK, Nevill Drury and Gregory Tillett. $9.95p ISBN 0-7100-8875-2, 248pp. ROU78. All the key areas are covered by this sourcebook including astrology, ESP, Kirlian photography, reincarnation, palmistry, faith healing, white magic and the Tarot. It is a well-researched compilation of knowledge in these areas.

ON ASTROLOGY, Peter Livingston. $1.95p ISBN 013-638833-7, 143pp. PRE75. Written primarily for children, the history of astrology and an analysis of astrological fundamentals such as the signs, houses and planets are presented with illustrations and in a language suitable for children or the beginning student.

OUR FATE AND THE ZODIAC, Margaret Mayo. $3.00s facsimile reprint (1900) 135pp. HEA.

PARALLEL IN ASTROLOGY, L. Furze-Morrish. $7.45p ISBN 0-914350-10-2, VUL75. This book by the famous Furze-Morrish, one of Australia's leading astrologers, discusses parallels in both natal and progressed horoscopes.

PARALLELS, Their Hidden Meaning, Charles Jayne. $7.50p ASB. Their effect by transit and progression is covered as well as their meaning in the natal chart. The tables are enlarged with parallels in synastry.

PARALLELS TO MIDHEAVEN AND ASCENDANT, King Keyes. $1.50p ISBN 0-87887-309-0, 8pp. CHU68. This short pamphlet shows how to calculate and interpret the parallel aspect which is made when a planet, Ascendant or the Midheaven mutually occupies the same degree of declination.

PART OF FIND, Marie R. Deleone. $8.95p ISBN 0-914350-48-X, VUL. The Part of Find was recently discovered without the aid of a computer. Ivy M. Goldstein-Jacobsen says"I always use the Part of Find in my charts." The Part of Find can be used in horary, natal or mundane astrology.

PASSION PLANETS: The Astrology of Relationships, Shellie Enteen and Judy Jacobs. $2.50p ISBN 05269-8, 288pp. JOV80. This book shows how to create a composite chart for a relationship by combining two horoscopes to form a third. It shows how Venus and Mars are guides to romance, how to find the best love partner or determine the future of a relationship, how love signs interact and how these planets affect one's ambitions, energies and love style.

PERSONAL ALCHEMY, C.C. Zain. $8.00p ISBN 0-87887-362-7, 320pp. CHU49. Zain's focus in this volume is shedding light on the path to enlightenment. He also prescribes stellar healing, or suggestions of what to eat when specific planets are afflicted.

PHRASES AND FRAGMENTS, E. Wilson. $5.50p AFA.

PIONEERS OF TOMORROW, Karen K. Spahn. $7.50p ASA80. This is an astrological history of the United States and Russian Space Programs from their inception to the present. It presents the facts and horoscopes for every rocket launch since Sputnik and Goddard's historic experiments. Includes the birth data of every American and Russian astronaut. Appendix includes a statistical analysis of the astronaut's Sun signs with birth data.

PLANETARIZATION OF CONSCIOUSNESS, Dane Rudhyar. $7.95p ISBN 0-88231-038-0, 320pp. ASI77. Rudhyar sees one society evolving through the worldwide interaction of all cultures. A new type of planetary consciousness will reveal the full human potential. This volume deals with the nature of humanity and develops a relationship to the present period and the consequences in the future.

PLANETARY CONTAINMENTS, John Sandbach and Ronn Ballard. $10.95p ISBN 0-930706-05-6, 330pp. SEK80. Based upon a technique by Volguine, the authors describe the influence of every planet in the horoscope according to the two planets which surround it. Nine hundred interpretations, instructions and examples are included.

PLANETARY HARMONIES: An Astrological Book of Meditation, Joan Hodgson. $12.95c ISBN 0-85487-046-6, 160pp. WHE/CRC80. Astrologically-based meditations are given in this book for each morning and evening of the week, and for new and full Moons throughout the year, which demonstrate how to live with the natural cycles in the year. The final chapter gives an astrological interpretation of the planes of consciousness. The study of meditation and astrology is presented as a way to self-healing and world-healing.

PLANETARY HOUR BOOK, Llewellyn George. $5.00p ISBN 0-87542-270-5, 217pp. LLE06. The planetary ruler of the given hour of a past event influences that event, according to the author. This theory has implications for electional astrology which locates the best time for a future event. Extensive tables are included showing the use of planetary rulers, information on the areas ruled by each of the planets, longitude and latitude tables and the correction factor for changing standard to mean time.

PLANETARY INFLUENCE AND THE HUMAN SOUL, Manly Palmer Hall. $1.75p ISBN 0-89314-341-3, 32pp. PHR57. This is a transcription of Hall's lecture on the spiritual basis of the science of astrology and the benefits of its study.

PLANETARY PATTERNS, Robert Carl Jansky. $8.00p 99pp. ASA74. A guide to the recognition and delineation of the eight basic chart patterns, and their significance in character analysis.

PLANETS AND HUMAN BEHAVIOR, Jeff Mayo. $4.20p ISBN 85243-268-2, 172pp. FOW72. Mayo correlates the Sun, Moon and planets to mental and emotional behavior in terms of both traditional and contemporary psychology. He uses Jungian concepts of psychic structure to synthesize a mass of associated ideas. Practical guidance is given with the help of an example birth chart.

PLANETS & ASTEROIDS, Esther V. Leinbach. $7.75p ISBN 0-914350-04-8, 248pp. VUL74. The planets and four largest asteroids are delineated in this text and their relationship to one another is examined via the conjunction aspect, whether natally or with another's chart (synastry). Case studies are included in the second edition.

PLANETS: COMPATIBILITY, Marc Robertson. $4.00p 52pp. AFA. Relationships, habits, sex and synastry factors are all discussed.

PLANETS IN ASPECT: Understanding Your Inner Dynamics, Robert Pelletier. $10.95p ISBN 0-914918-20-6, 364pp. PAR74. Pelletier explores aspects, the planetary relationships that describe our individual energy patterns, and how we can integrate them into our lives. Every major aspect-conjunction, sextile, square, trine, opposition and inconjunct is covered.

PLANETS IN COMPOSITE: Analyzing Human Relationships, Robert Hand. $12.95p ISBN 0-914918-22-2, 362pp. PAR75. In Hand's book on the astrology of human relationships, he explains the technique of the composite chart, combining two individual's charts to create a third chart of the relationship itself and how to interpret it. Case studies are presented plus twelve chapters of delineations of composite Sun, Moon and planets in all houses and major aspects.

PLANETS IN HOUSES: Experiencing Your Environment, Robert Pelletier. $12.95p ISBN 0-914918-27-3, 366pp. PAR78. Pelletier brings the ancient art of natal horoscope interpretation into a new era of accuracy, concreteness and richness of detail. He delineates the meaning of each planet as derived by counting from each of the twelve houses and in relation to the outer houses with which it forms trines, sextiles, squares and oppositions, inconjuncts and semi-sextiles. Seventeen different house relationships are delineated for each planet in each house, 2184 delineations in all.

PLANETS IN LOVE: Exploring Your Emotional and Sexual Needs, John Townley. $12.95c ISBN 0-914918-11-7, 368pp. PAR78. Townley takes an unabashed look at human sexuality and the different kinds of relationships that people form to meet their various emotional and sexual needs. An intimate astrological analysis of sex and love, with five hundred fifty interpretations of each planet in every possible sign, house and aspect. Sexual behavior is discussed according to mental, emotional and spiritual areas of development.

PLANETS IN MUTUAL RECEPTION, Anne Ryan. $5.95p 108pp. HOU80. The author discusses three types of mutual receptions that may be found in a natal horoscope: two planets in each other's signs, two planets falling in each other's houses and a third type which is a combination of house and sign. The problems of mutual receptions stem from the houses the planets rule and manifest in the houses of the midpoint.

PLANETS IN TRANSIT: Life Cycles for Living, Robert Hand. $18.95p ISBN 0-914918-24-9, 524pp. PAR76. This is a psychological approach to astrological prediction and includes delineations of the Sun, Moon and each planet transiting each natal house and forming each aspect to the natal Sun, Moon, planets, Ascendant and Midheaven. Includes introductory chapters on the theory and applications of transits.

PLANETS IN YOUTH: Patterns of Early Development, Robert Hand. $12.95p ISBN 0-914918-26-5, 367pp. PAR77. Parents can use this book to help their children cope with the complexities of growing up, and readers of all ages can use it to understand themselves and their own patterns of early development. Introductory chapters discuss parent-child relationships and planetary energies in children's charts. All important horoscope factors are delineated stressing possibilities rather than certainties.

PLANETS-WHAT THEY MEAN, Paul G. Clancy. $1.50p 12pp. CLA61. This is a collection of the author's writings on the subject of planetary meanings and how they are modified by sign, house placement and aspects in the natal chart.

PLANET VULCAN: HISTORY, NATURE, TABLES, L.H. Weston. $2.50p 35pp. AFA. This reprint of an early work contains tables for calculating Vulcan's heliocentric and geocentric longitude. It also includes a history and a brief introduction to the planets said to be within the orbit of Mercury.

PLUTO, Pat Benis Miller. $3.50p 54pp. MAC. This illuminating look at Pluto and its significance in the natal chart discusses astrological symbols and essence, cycles, reincarnation and karma, sign and house position, and includes many interesting poems.

What leading astrologers say about Horoscope Symbols

Neil Michelsen

"*Horoscope Symbols* should be on your must reading list. Rob Hand's rare combination of technical mastery and interpretive insight are what make him the most brilliant astrologer of our generation."

Alan Oken

"As usual his writing is very clear, and what is most noteworthy is his ability to synthesize his comprehensive understanding of astrology from his basic scientific viewpoint and relate this in humanistic prose. The chapters on midpoints are especially valuable."

Noel Tyl

"As a guide to perception, astrology needs constant refreshment and creative scrutiny. We can always be grateful for the incisive and energetic views offered by Robert Hand."

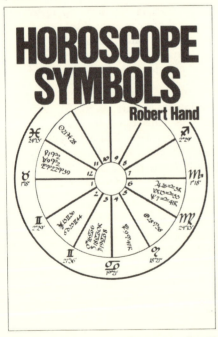

ISBN 0-914918-16-8   371 pages $14.95

Lois Rodden

"With one of the finest minds in astrology today, Rob Hand explores the symbols of our study in a book to be savored by student and professional alike."

Charles Emerson

"At last, a new work which ennobles the literature of astrology! Rob Hand leads the student along familiar tracks in a voyage of thrilling rediscovery . . . he sharpens our own perceptions and nourishes our deeper understanding. Rare indeed must be the reader, whether neophyte or practiced professional, who fails to develop a better grasp of the infinite complex of astrology through careful study of *Horoscope Symbols*."

Tracy Marks

"Robert Hand grasps the essential meanings of astrological symbols and presents them with psychological depth and constructive guidance."

Betty Lundsted

"Robert Hand has produced another gem! As always he's well-spoken, understandable and informative. His work has helped thousands of students get a grasp of the symbols of modern astrology."

and Robert Hand

"Many modern attempts to do what I have done in this book have contradicted some of the traditional meanings and ended up clouding rather than clarifying things. I often prefer the older descriptions because, despite their superficial and fatalistic style, they seem closer to the archetypes that I believe are embodied in astrology. I believe that the primary value of astrology is as a symbolic description of the human psyche. I hope that this book will spur you on to similar efforts to understand the basic symbols of astrology."

Available at your local bookstore
Published by Para Research, Whistlestop Mall, Rockport, MA 01966

PLUTO, Fritz Brunhubner. $5.50c 93pp. AFA34. This volume, now translated from German, was written soon after Pluto was discovered and is still considered an important work. The results of the author's research document Pluto's mythological and astronomical context and support his explanations of Pluto's character and influence in the astrological chart. Sample delineations and information on aspects are included.

PLUTO, Laurel Lowell. $4.75p 105pp. LLE73. Pluto is delineated through the signs, houses and charts with Pluto's aspects organized by planets. Transits, Plutonian correspondences and a Pluto ephemeris for 1851 to 2000 are included.

PLUTO: FROM DARKNESS INTO LIGHT, Tracy Marks. $2.50p 19pp. SAG. Marks focuses upon characteristic Plutonian experiences of death and rebirth, energy release and the issue of power and powerlessness to increase understanding of the psychological experience of Pluto, whether natally or by transit, and of how to harness its powerful energy.

PLUTO IN LIBRA, Manly Palmer Hall. $1.75p ISBN 0-89314-342-1, 31pp. PHR71. Pluto is analyzed and Pluto in Libra is interpreted with special emphasis placed on the meaning of this influence for both the individual person and the United States.

PLUTO, NEPTUNE AND PISCES DUALITY, Germaine Holley. $3.95p 150pp. WEI74. Holley's detailed study concludes that Pisces is ruled by Pluto and Neptune jointly and analyzes their role in the horoscope. She gives a complete aspectarian for Neptune and Pluto in addition to delineating their meanings in the signs and houses and analyzing Pisces on the house cusps. A final section explores the placement of Pluto and Neptune in the charts of the United States, Egypt and Israel.

PLUTONIAN PHOENIX, Dale Richardson. $6.50p 166pp. AFA74. This collection of the author's published articles from the last fifteen years, including an appendix of recent additions, covers an assortment of subjects, most of which relate to Pluto and its transits. Many of the articles note the effect of Pluto on some individuals and public events.

POTENTIAL FULFILLED: Vol I, Accident Patterns, Priscilla Gilbert. $4.50p 105pp. AFA76. In the first volume of this two-part study on accident patterns, case studies and accompanying charts document the author's findings.

POTENTIAL FULFILLED: Vol II, What Saved Them?, Priscilla Gilbert. $4.50p 100pp. AFA76. The second volume concentrates on the charts and case studies of those who did not meet tragic ends.

POWER OF FIXED STARS, Joseph E. Rigor. $11.95p; $15.95c 480pp. ASP80. This volume, representing the results of twenty-five years of research, communicates an understanding of the influence of the fixed stars on behavior. A fixed star ephemeris from 1800 to 2030 is included as well as six hundred influences applied to nativities; exact magnitudes and longitudes of two hundred fifty-three fixed stars; modifying effect of the Moon and explanations of psychic ability and of violence; and the effects of nebulae and clusters.

POWER OF PLUTO, Arlene Robertson and Margaret Wilson. $7.95p ISBN 0-930-706-02-1, 240pp. SEK79. A thorough examination of the influence, personal meaning and world effect of Pluto, the planet of transformation and rebirth. Includes interpretations of natal aspects to Pluto as well as progressions and transits both to and from this mysterious planet.

POWER TRIO: MARS, JUPITER, SATURN, Mae R. Wilson-Ludlam. $6.95p 152pp. MAC76. This is a companion piece to INTERPRET YOUR CHART, but complete in itself. It follows Mars, Jupiter and Saturn through the signs, houses and aspects with keyword phraseology. The quincunx is explained and Saturn is studied through the intrinsic square. The book ends with a look at the coming Aquarian Age.

PRACTICAL ASTROLOGY, Alan Leo. $5.00s facsimile reprint (1911) 224pp. HEA. Leo explores esoteric astrology and uses many illustrative charts in this small but comprehensive astrology text.

PRACTICAL ASTROLOGY, Comte de Saint-Germain. $3.95p ISBN 0-87877-018-6; $9.95c ISBN 0-87877-318-5, 257pp. NCP01. Saint-Germain, the famous nineteenth century occultist and writer, presents the basics of astrology and chart erection. He also explores the relationship between the Tarot and astrology.

PRACTICAL ASTROLOGY, Vivian Robson. $3.95p 184pp. WEI30. This somewhat old-fashioned manual of basic astrology, first published in 1930, teaches horoscope calculation and delineation, relying heavily on physical types and keywords. The final section gives instructions for calculating and interpreting progressions.

PRECISE PROGRESSED CHARTS, Mohan Koparkar. $4.95p ISBN 0-918922-03-8, 105pp. MOH76. Koparkar discusses the basic mechanism of event formation in a chart which he calls the Precise Progressed Chart. The book describes the potential, principle and culminating structure of an event. The mechanics of the technique are first explained and then a set of eleven sample charts are fully analyzed. Hindu astrology is influential on the ideas presented here.

PREDICTING WITH INSTANT ASTROLOGY, Mary Orser and Rick and Glory Brightfield. $4.95p ISBN 0-06-090572-7, HAR77. Personal and political predictions can be made using this simple method. A full series of tables and graphs are included.

PREDICTIVE ASTROLOGY, Frances Sakoian and Louis Acker. $12.95c ISBN 0-06-013744-4, 448pp. HAR77. This book is a consolidation of the authors' previously published work on tansits. Additional material is provided on the symbolism of the planets, signs, houses, and the role of aspects.

PREFACE TO PRENATAL CHARTS, Charles Jayne. $6.00p ASB75. This much expanded second edition has fresh material on a whole new arcane astrology and cosmic centers. Jayne presents some conclusions of his research into prenatal astrology with seven illustrative charts. He presents his main thesis that charts can be created for the different stages of the"Descent of the Soul" into the body.

PRENATAL EPOCH, E.H. Bailey. $6.95c 239pp. WEI70. First published in 1916, this work shows how prenatal charts can be used to ascertain birthtimes for rectification of natal charts. Bailey also shows how these charts relate to twins, prenatal abnormalities and infant mortality. Examples of converse and primary directions tie prenatal charts to life events used for rectification purposes. For professionals and advanced students.

PRIMER FOR NATAL CHART, Holiday. $9.50p AFA.

PRIMER FOR SECONDARY PROGRESSIONS, Holiday. $6.50p AFA.

PRINCIPLES OF ASTROLOGICAL GEOMANCY, Franz Hartmann. $3.00s facsimile reprint 100pp. HEA. Divination by punctuation.

PRINCIPLES OF DEPTH ASTROLOGY, Tracy Marks. $3.00p 30pp. SAG. In this book the principles of humanistic and spiritual astrology are related to a variety of psychological and spiritual discoveries of modern science.

PRINCIPLES OF SYNASTRY, Henry Weingarten. $5.00p ISBN 0-88231-100-X, pp. ASI. This clear presentation of the basic principles and working techniques of synastry is suitable for the beginning or more advanced astrology student. This study highlights many important areas previously neglected in the relationship chart by the effect of locational astrology on marriage, the"list condition," marriage triangles, contract therapy and more.

PROFILES OF WOMEN, Lois M. Rodden. $15.00p 368pp. AFA. Horoscopes and biographical resumes of three hundred famous women through five hundred years of history are represented in the twelve signs of the zodiac.

PROGRESSED HOROSCOPE, Alan Leo. $6.95p ISBN 0-89281-180-3, 328pp. INT/WEI69. Leo's comprehensive guide to a system of predicting the future completely outlines methods for drawing up annual forecasts. Included are detailed delineations of every possible progressed aspect, solar, mutual, and lunar, and their influence on character and destiny. He also includes a lengthy chapter treating exoteric and esoteric aspects.

PROGRESSED HOROSCOPE SIMPLIFIED, Leigh Hope Milburn. $6.00c 170pp. AFA28. A comprehensive text on the progressed horoscope, giving practical guidance and help with reading the chart.

PROGRESSION FORMULAS, King Keyes. $2.00p 12pp. AFA75."It is difficult to find clear rules with examples of problems that come up in progressions. For this reason, I have written this little booklet in hopes it may solve some of these problems. I have concentrated on ten examples only, using a Raphael's Ephemeris for noon and Dalton's Table of Houses."

PROGRESSIONS AND DIRECTIONS, Charles Jayne. $6.00p 53pp. ASB73. This four-part book gives very technical information on secondary or major, minor and tertiary progressions; solar arcs; primary directions and symbolic directions. Double interpolations are explained in the appendix.

PROGRESSIONS, DIRECTIONS AND RECTIFICATION, Zipporah P. Dobyns. $4.00p 100pp. TIA75. In this humanistic study of the major current pattern systems, Dr. Dobyns defines secondary, tertiary and minor directions, solar arc directions and transits. She discusses how they can be used in the rectification process. The charts of Edward, John and Robert Kennedy are used to illustrate progressions, directions and rectification.

PROGRESSIONS IN ACTION, Doris Chase Doane. $9.50p 243pp. AFA77. Doane demonstrates her progression techniques with the charts of twenty-one famous actors, actresses and other well-known figures. This is a basic tool for studying the Hermetic system of progressions.

PSYCHOANALYZING THE TWELVE ZODIACAL TYPES, Manly Palmer Hall. $1.75p ISBN 0-89314-346-4, 64pp. PHR37. Hall analyses each of the twelve Sun signs.

PSYCHOLOGICAL ASTROLOGY, David Goodman and Catherine T. Grant. $4.00p 55pp. AFA74. The temperament of each of the twelve signs is described and illustrated with a number of sample charts and case studies.

PSYCHOLOGY OF THE PLANETS, Francoise Gauquelin. $7.95p ISBN 0-917086-32-5, 128pp. AST81. Gauquelin has summarized the most significant and verifiable astrological findings of this century. She notes the differences between traditional and modern astrology, and discusses the ninth and twelfth houses in detail.

PTOLEMY'S TETRABIBLOS (Quadripartite), trans. J.M. Ashmand. $6.00s fascimile reprint (1917) 240pp. HEA. These four books on the influence of the stars are translated from the Greek Paraphrase of Proculs. This is one of the older, rarer books on astrology.

PURSUIT OF DESTINY, Muriel Bruce Hasbrouck. $1.95p INN. The author discusses para-astrology which is a synthesis of astrology and the Tarot.

PSYCHOLOGY OF PROGRESSIONS, Lynn G. Dalton. $11.95p ISBN 0-914350-08-0, VUL80. This book uses the equal-house method in a gestalt approach to secondary progressions, with many examples and case studies.

RADIX SYSTEM, Vivian Robson. $5.75p 110pp. DAR74. The author develops and extends Sepharial's system of approximating an astrological chart's direction of progress. She demonstrates the radix system by explaining and giving reference material on the different types of directions and the nature of midpoints, parallels and converse directions. There is an analysis of the effects of directions through the planets and signs.

RAPHAEL'S HORARY ASTROLOGY, Raphael. $2.00p facsimile reprint (1897) 103pp. HEA. A book written exclusively on horary, the branch of astrology that answers questions about the future by casting a chart for the exact moment the question is formulated in the mind.

RAPHAEL'S MUNDANE ASTROLOGY, Raphael. $1.20p ISBN 0-572-00247-5, 205pp. WFO. Raphael evaluates the effects of the planets and signs upon nations and countries and classifies the parts of the body by house.

RECENT ADVANCES IN NATAL ASTROLOGY: A Critical Review 1900-1976, Geoffrey Dean. $25.00p 598pp. REC77. Dean asserts that "astrology has a vast burgeoning literature in which the same basic untruths are endlessly recycled, most 'research' is technically incompetent and is aimed not at clarifying but at justifying tradition." He then reviews those few studies that meet his rigorous standards. A clear, concise and complete work of scholarship by Dean and an international team of collaborators.

RECTIFICATION OF THE BIRTH TIME, Gustave Schwickert. $4.50p 163pp. AFA54. An explanation of the technique of rectification when the birthtime is unknown.

REINCARNATION THROUGH THE ZODIAC, Joan Hodgson. $4.95p ISBN 0-916360-11-3, 137pp. CRC43. A study of the signs of the zodiac from the perspective of reincarnation. The author is the founder of the White Eagle School of Astrology which emphasizes a spiritual and esoteric approach to this ancient science.

RELATING, AN ASTROLOGICAL GUIDE FOR LIVING WITH OTHERS ON A SMALL PLANET, Liz Greene. $7.95p ISBN 0-87728-373-7, 289pp. WEI78. An astrological guide to living with others on a small planet. Provocative and original analysis within a framework of Jungian psychology shows the ways in which people relate on both conscious and unconscious levels. The author respects the many differences among human beings, and rejects narrow judgements of "normal" and "abnormal."

RELATION OF THE MINERAL SALTS OF THE BODY TO THE SIGNS OF THE ZODIAC, combined with ROAD TO THE MOON, George Carey and Inez E. Perry. 2.50p facsimile reprint (1932) HEA.

RELATIONSHIPS AND LIFE CYCLES, Stephen Arroyo. $6.95p ISBN 0-916360-12-1, 224pp. CRC79. Concerning some of the key areas of modern astrology, this book is actually a collection of workshops on three major subjects; determining the individual's capacity and need for relationships by studying the birth chart; understanding any specific relationship by comparing two birth charts; and using transits and planetary cycles practically and intelligently.

HOLD THE STARS
IN YOUR HAND

The symbols of Astrology do not have to be tied to actual Heavenly Bodies. Roll our twelve-sided dice and you will get the one house-sign-planet combination (out of 1728 possible combinations) that presents the answer to your question. Use the complete instruction book provided to interpret the answer—it's easy!

LINDA GOODMAN, Author of "Sun Signs", "Love Signs" and "Venus Trines at Midnight" rarely gives endorsements and accepts no money for them. Here's what "the world's most popular Astrologer" says:

"Astro-Dice is a game. Why not? Life itself is a kind of game. But whether this is just another Astrological parlor trick—or a valuable growing tool for the spirit—depends on no-one but yourself. You alone control its function. Astro-Dice can be an amazing aid to intuition, or an empty, meaningless novelty. As with the I Ching, there is here a potential link to the pulsing Synchronicity of the Universe, capable of bringing startling insight—sudden illumination—when used with the proper attitude of inquiry. When the need to know is deep and genuine, the answers will be channelled symbolically and with certainty from a wise Universe, tuned in to your own Higher Self in perfect harmony, at any given moment of time. Approach Astro-Dice with humility and thoughtfulness, and your reward will be personal enlightment. However, foolish questions, motivated simply by shallow curiosity, will just as surely receive confusing and misleading answers. Ever has it been—and ever shall it be—that Heaven turns a deaf ear toward the frivolous seeker, searching only for temporary pleasure or instant knowledge for use of personal gain."

DR. MARC EDMUND JONES
"Dean of American Astrologers"
" . . . just about the most novel and sheerly clever contribution to the games that man plays since perhaps back into unknown antiquity."

DANE RUDHYAR
Founder of "Holistic Astrology"
"A simple and instructive way — if not abused — of satisfying the longing of human beings for oracular answers to their unanswerable questions."

DORIS GREAVES
Leading Australian Astrologer
"This is a simple way to learn the symbols of Astrology. It develops intuition, gives clear and concise answers and is lots of fun for anyone."

F. RICHARD NOLLE
Reviewer for Dell Horoscope Magazine, comments: *" . . . It sounds like heresy, but I have seen it work."*

TRACY MARKS
The reaction of Tracy Marks, highly-respected New England Astrologer, was: *"What a Discovery!"*

Get on board now with the Oracle of the Century! NAT. PHENCO, INC.
Gladstone Station Box 10724
Kansas City, Mo. 64118
James R. Gross Astrology Director (PMAFA)

Available at your local bookstore

Produced by K.C. School of the Occult, Box 25421, K.C., Mo. 64119 (J.R. Gross - Pres)

RELATIVE STRENGTH OF SIGNS AND PLANETS, Colin James III. $12.95c 273pp. COL78.

RETROGRADES, Mohan Koparkar. $5.95p ISBN 0-918922-07-0, 144pp. MOH80. In this book, the author presents a new approach to retrograde planets by way of the opposition aspect, which is closely related to the phenomenon of retrogradation. Topics include retrogrades through each house, house rulerships, transits, progressions, mundane astrology, combinations, interceptions and reincarnation.

REVOLUTIONIZING ASTROLOGY WITH HELIOCENTRIC, T. Patrick Davis. $9.00p 132pp. DAV80. The author asserts that these new heliocentric discoveries affect every phase of astrological practice.

RHYTHM OF HUMAN FULFILLMENT, Dane Rudhyar. $2.50p ISBN 0-916108-02-3, 96pp. SEE73. Rudhyar expands the vision of an emerging new society and world, urging us to move beyond the known. Broad, all-encompassing principles are laid out based on the cyclic nature of time, a holistic view of existance and man's place within it.

RISING SIGNS, Carolyn Dodson. $8.00p 111pp. DOD. This is a compendium on each of the signs of the zodiac as they appear on the Ascendant of the horoscope, illustrated with sixty caricatures.

RULER OF THE NATIVITY, Alexandre Volguine. $6.95c ISBN 0-88231-001-0, 132pp. ASI73. In Volguine's modern treatment of the Almuten or birth governor, the ruler of the nativity, he asserts that it represents the strongest planet in the horoscope. In this system, the strength of each planet, sign, house, aspect and so forth is found and assigned a series of coefficients derived from astronomical and astrological criteria.

RULERSHIP BOOK, Rex E. Bills. $12.50c 438pp. MAC71. This practical book contains an alphabetical listing of the rulerships of the planets, signs and houses over everything on Earth and every facet of our lives. There is also an appendix with special listings of the rulers of the principal bones, vertebrae, muscles and veins of the body. Blank pages are provided for the reader's own findings.

SABIAN BOOK, Marc Edmund Jones. $13.50c ISBN 0-87878-013-0, 400pp. AFA73. This is a collection of letters directed to the students of the Sabian Assembly, illustrating the Sabian vision of restoring the solar mysteries. The letters deal with the integrity of man and his existence in this world.

SABIAN MANUAL, Marc Edmund Jones. $10.50c ISBN 0-87878-010-6, 288pp. AFA57. This modern introduction to Eternal Wisdom is also a manual of guidance along the "Solar Path." The rituals of the Sabian Assembly are described as illuminating a way toward spiritual fulfillment.

SABIAN SYMBOLS IN ASTROLOGY, Marc Edmund Jones. $5.95p ISBN 0-394-73579-X, 437pp. SHA53; $13.50c ISBN 0-87878-009-2, 448pp. AFA. This is a comprehensive guide to the Sabian symbols, astrological metaphors of human experience associated with the three hundred sixty degrees of the Zodiac. The Sabian symbols provide a way to identify and understand nature's cycles and human character. They give insight into the significance and nature of almost any human situation or relationship.

SATURN, A NEW LOOK AT AN OLD DEVIL, Liz Greene. $4.50p ISBN 0-87728-306-0, 196pp. WEI76. Liz Greene shatters the myth of Saturn as a "malefic" planet and pierces the veil of obscurity that has shrouded this planet for centuries, successfully bringing to light the true meaning of Saturn experience. This well-written text includes chapters on Saturn in each of the signs and houses, and Saturn's aspects in birth chart and in synastry.

SATURN, THE REAPER, Alan Leo. $2.50p 108pp. WEI73. In this 1916 series of lectures, Leo discusses how Saturn symbolism ties into the Hindu pantheon, karma, dharma, Saturn in the role of reaper, Saturn as indicator of time, limitation and maturity, and Saturn as the bridge between higher and lower self. The serious student will appreciate the depth and breadth of the lectures.

SCIENCE OF FOREKNOWLEDGE, Sepharial. $3.50s facsimile reprint (1918) 160pp. HEA. Sepharial introduces and discusses ancient Hindu and Hebrew astrology, explores the nature of Lilith and Neptune, and evaluates the radix system as a means for doing predictions.

SCIENTIFIC BASIS OF ASTROLOGY, Michel Gauquelin. $3.95p ISBN 0-8128-1350-2, 255pp. STE69. Gauquelin's work has made a Time cover story and is taken seriously by many American scientists. Astrobiology is documented with scientific experiments showing that extraterrestrial forces do affect life on earth. The author examines Jung's differentiation between astrological and parapsychological conditions.

SCOPE OF ASTROLOGICAL PREDICTION, Marc Edmund Jones. $16.50c ISBN 0-87878-012-2, 461pp. AFA69. This comprehensive exposition of the dynamic horoscope explains not only the most familiar form of horoscopic progression, the technique of secondary directions, but also primary and tertiary directions. Rectification procedures and solar and lunar returns are also discussed.

SECONDARY PROGRESSIONS, Laurel Lowell. $4.75p 96pp. MAC73. Secondary Progressions operate on the theory that the day of birth represents the First Progressed Year, the day after birth represents the Second Progressed Year, and so on through the life cycle. With charts and example work sheets this is a quick and accurate reference for locating the adjusted calculation date and interpreting its use in relation to predictive work with Seconday Progressions.

SELECTED TOPICS IN ASTROLOGY, Robert Carl Jansky. $8.00p ASA74. This intermediate textbook attempts to answer some of the most commonly-asked questions about special horoscope phenomena. Formulated in ten lessons, it covers such things as focal determinators, quadrature emphasis, the planet in oriental appearance, retrogrades, intercepted signs, and stelliums. Its appendix references example charts of these phenomena in the book ASTROLOGY-HERE AND NOW.

SELF-DISCOVERY THROUGH ASTROLOGY, Terrye Lang. $7.95p ISBN 0-914350-24-2, VUL80. This basic book emphasizes the self-discovery approach.

SEVENTY-FIVE WINDOWS, F.S. Pounds. $7.00p AFA. Medical astrology.

SEX AND THE OUTER PLANETS, Barbara Watters. $4.95p 222pp. AFA71. An unusual, authoritative book for the advanced astrologer.

SEX AND THE PLANETS, Sylvia Sherman. $1.00p AMS67.

SEX AND THE STARS, Penticost. $2.25p ISBN 0-553-13444-2, 196pp. BAN73. Penticost describes the twelve Sun signs for men and women and the one hundred forty-four combinations.

SEX, MIND, HABIT COMPATIBILITY, Marc Robertson. $3.00p ACN75. Robertson discloses his method for determining human compatibility based on an evaluation of astrological factors present in the birth charts of two people.

SEXUAL ASSAULTS: PRE-IDENTIFYING THOSE VULNERABLE, T. Patrick Davis. $8.00p $10.25c DAV. Forty case histories show how to interpret the natal chart to astrologically recognize if a person is vulnerable to sexual attack. This research report is innovative and responsibly presented.

SEXUAL BEHAVIOR IN THE ZODIAC, Chauncey D. King. $3.00p 46pp. AFA. The author shows how to use the Sun sign as the indicator and gives instructions for using the placement of Mercury, fifth house and twelfth house.

SIDE LIGHTS OF ASTROLOGY, Thyrza Escobar. $4.00p ISBN 0-912368-02-0, 60pp. GOL. This book includes an extensive astro-language vocabulary and techniques that reveal the birth-map and its unfoldment. A clear explanation is given of the significant "Y" technique originated by Carl Leipert.

SIDEREAL HANDBOOK, James A. Eshelman. $4.00p 50pp. STY/ASA75. Revised ASA81. There are explanations and examples for calculating fourteen different sidereal predictive techniques. The calculations are demonstrated using logs and motion tables.

SIGNS AND PARTS IN PLAIN ENGLISH, Press and Ima Roberts, and Don Borkowski. $7.45p ISBN 0-914350-12-9, 156pp. VUL76. This second book in the authors' "in plain English" series is written in down-to-earth, easy-to-understand language. It covers Arabic parts, intercepted signs, retrograde planets, cusps, chart patterns and shapes, the elements, empty signs, eclipses and psychic qualities in the horoscope.

SIGNS OF LOVE, Jeraldine Saunders. $2.50p 320pp. PIN77. This is a personal Sun sign guide to love and sexual compatibility.

We Publish Books, Too!

. . . The Best In Astrology From The People Who Made America Astrology Conscious . . . .

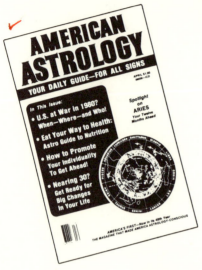

The same publisher who has brought you **American Astrology** for over 49 years has books, too! Our growing list of titles includes some of astrology's most readable authors writing on timely and interesting subjects. Book buyers like them because they're informative, entertaining and just plain good reading, while booksellers like them because their exposure in the pages of a large-circulation astrology monthly makes them sought after by the book-buying public. Check out these big sellers from our list:

Jupiter Through the Signs
by Frederic van Norstrand

A popular writer takes a thorough look at the mythology and symbolism of Jupiter, then traces its meaning through each of the twelve signs. The broad appeal of this little book reaches from the professional astrologer, who will find it enriches his interpretations of Jupiter in the birth chart, to the casual buyer of astrology books. A handy table in the back of the book gives the sign positions of Jupiter from 1900 to 2000. Paper, $4.25.

Taking the Kid Gloves off Astrology
by Garth Allen

Six years and several printings after its first publication in book form, demand for this book has increased with time. Garth Allen uses his wit and lively style to take the reader on a journey into the hidden depths of psychological meaning underlying planetary symbolism, discussing each of the planets—Mercury through Pluto—at length. Makes the planets come alive! Paper, $3.25.

The Solunars Handbook
by Cyril Fagan

Did astrology take a wrong turn way back when? Cyril Fagan spent many years explaining his often-controversial ideas on the way astrology was, and what it could be in his popular "Solunars" series in *American Astrology*. From the zodiac, to the houses, to the elementary symbolism of the planets, this selection from that series explains Fagan's ideas in a way that is entertaining, stimulating and always challenging! Paper, $5.35.

Available at your local bookstore.

Clancy Publications, Inc.   **2505 N. Alvernon Way**   **Tucson, Arizona 85712**

SIGNS OF THE ZODIAC, Chauncey D. King. $3.00p 109pp. AFA. This is a clear and simple presentation of the study of the twelve Sun signs in relation to the individual.

SIGNS OF THE ZODIAC ANALYZED, Isabelle M. Pagan. $6.50p ISBN 0-7229-5102-7, 318pp. THE69. Formerly published under the title FROM PIONEER TO POET, this matter-of-fact analysis of the twelve zodiacal signs is illustrated by the birth charts of historic figures.

SILVER KEY, Sepharial. $3.00s 94pp. HEA. The accuracy of astrological prediction is tested on horse racing. Detailed instructions and tables are provided.

SIMPLIFIED ASTRONOMY FOR ASTROLOGERS, David Williams. $5.00p 88pp. AFA. A review of the precession of the equinoxes throughout history. The author astrologically interprets the events from each age and explores the development of astrological techniques.

SIMPLIFIED HORARY ASTROLOGY, Ivy M. Goldstein-Jacobson. $11.00c 278pp. GOJ60. Horary charts are drawn up for the moment a question takes form consciously. The author shows how to use horary astrology to answer queries about personal problems, family, marriage, health, business, travel, finances, children and hundreds of other issues, with thirty-four detailed examples to illustrate the method.

SIMPLIFIED SCIENTIFIC EPHEMERIS, $1.50p each 1857 to 1999; $7.00p 10-year volumes: 1880-89 to 1990-99 ROS. These ephemerides indicate new and full Moons, eclipses, Moon's nodes, longitudes, declinations and a twenty-four hour table of logarithms and latitudes from 1923. From 1936 it also gives a daily aspectarian, the time of entrance of the Sun and Moon into each sign and the monthly position of Pluto.

600 PERSONALITIES OF THE AQUARIUS, Jacques de Lescaut. $15.00p 102pp. EDI80. The birth information for six hundred Aquarian Europeans and Americans are listed in this compendium.

SOLAR AND LUNAR RETURNS, Donald A. Bradley. $3.95p ISBN 0-87542-045-1, 123pp. LLE74. Advanced students will appreciate this introduction to the fixed zodiac of sidereal astrology which the author contends is more accurate than tropical astrology. He bases his position on documentation using solar and lunar return charts which predict events for the coming solar or lunar year. Instructions and examples are included for casting the charts as well as an ephemeris of the Vernal Point for reference.

SOLAR RETURN BOOK OF PREDICTION, Raymond A. Merriman. $5.00p ISBN 0-930706-00-5, 132pp. SEK77. An informational presentation on calculating and interpreting solar returns. The author discusses both mundane activities and spiritual growth as influenced by the guiding light of the Sun.

SOLAR RETURNS, Cummings. $7.00p AFA81.

SOLUNARS HANDBOOK, Cyril Fagan. $5.35p 130pp. CLA76. This selection is from some of Fagan's best articles published in American Astrology Magazine. The meanings of the Sidereal Constellations, chart comparisons, prediction techniques, quotidians, aspects in solar and lunar return charts and mundoscopes are all discussed.

SOME MYSTERIES OF ASTROLOGY, Mary Elsnau. $4.00p HEA.

SOME PRINCIPLES OF HOROSCOPIC DELINEATION, Charles E.O. Carter. $5.25p 76pp. HUG. This instructive book is a companion piece to ASTROLOGICAL ASPECTS and follows PRINCIPLES OF ASTROLOGY.

SPHERES OF DESTINY, Michel Gauquelin. $15.75c 262pp. DEN80. Sub-titled Your Personality and the Planets, this is Gauquelin's answer to those who dismiss his statistical work in astrology as purely academic. This is a practical teaching manual written to show how the writer's findings on the personality traits can be applied.

SPHERICAL ASTRONOMY FOR ASTROLOGERS, George Noonan. $3.00p 62pp. AFA74. Noonan gives examples of formulae used in astrology for computing the Ascendant and Midheaven.

SPIRAL OF LIFE, Jinni Meyer and Joanne Wickenburg. $6.95p SEA. The demonstrated method in this volume, for understanding the personality through the birth chart, not only shows in concrete detail how to become aware of the direction and potential of the chart, but how the unconscious mind affects this potential and where integration is needed.

SPIRITUAL ASTROLOGY, C.C. Zain. $9.00p ISBN 0-87887-360-0, 416pp. CHU. Zain asserts that the meanings of the constellations are associated with every story in the Bible and all sacred spiritual books. The author includes illustrations for each of the forty-eight traditional constellations and dominant personality traits for every sign.

STARS, L. Edward Johndro. $6.95p 120pp. WEI73. This book concerns the relation of the latitudinal positions of the stars to personal or world events as well as periods of prosperity, depression and other cycles.

STARS & STOVES, AN ASTROLOGICAL COOKBOOK, Barbara Morbidoni. $5.00p ISBN 0-933646-06-2, 92pp. ARI. The foods, flavors and spices ruled by each sign are discussed and recipes given for a complete dinner, birthday cake and "celebrity" specialty for each zodiac sign.

STAR SIGNS FOR LOVERS, Liz Greene. $14.95c ISBN 0-8128-2765-1, 480pp. STE80. Love relationships are the theme of this book. The Sun sign or astrological signature is interpreted to better understand the complex and subtle patterns that form the personality and its approach to love.

STARS OF THE BIBLE, E.C. Mathews. $10.00c 162pp. MOT. The science of astrology is traced back through the Bible to prehistoric times. The author cites hundreds of related Bible quotations and gives astrological analyses. A main feature of the book is the eighty full page illustrations of the Bible by Gustav Dore.

STAR WHEEL TECHNIQUE, Thyrza Escobar. $12.00p ISBN 0-912368-17-9, GOL. This simple method devised by Carl Leipert shows how to make and interpret the natal star wheel and a composite that includes a flat chart, solar-equilibrium and radix in the solar chart, how to find and use star wheel cycles in life projections and/or to find personal activation for dates of events and which transits and/or progressions are in "open gates" for personal impact.

STELLAR HEALING, C.C. Zain. $7.95p ISBN 0-87887-355-4, 384pp. CHU47. The birth chart and progressed constants are given for one hundred sixty of the most prevalent diseases as well as the indicated stellar treatment.

STELLAR-NUMEROLOGY, Martita Tracy. $3.50p 44pp. HEA. This astrological interpretation of the alphabet is based on the Hebrew Kabala. Offset pages, typewritten format.

STOWE'S BIBLE ASTROLOGY, Lyman E. Stowe. $5.00s facsimile reprint (1907) 250pp. HEA. The twelve signs of the zodiac.

STRESS AND THE SUN SIGNS, Rupert Sewell. $4.95p ISBN 0-85030-241-2, 96pp. AQU/WEI81. This astrological guide to the self-treatment of stress, tension and anxiety includes a unique list of personality tendencies, arranged according to birthdate.

STUDENTS ASTROLOGICAL MANUAL, A. LeRoi Simmons. $2.00p ISBN 0-9605126-3-2 AQB76. This beginner's manual gives a complete, step-by-step method for erecting an accurate horoscope and interpreting it. Features include keywords, symbols and abbreviations, a detailed example chart, a page from an ephemeris and a table of houses, logarithm tables with detailed instructions, a blank chart form and a map showing the latest time zone changes.

STUDIES IN ASTROLOGY, Elman Bacher. $1.50p each or $12.50 set 96pp. ROS. Nine volumes. This series is composed of individual articles which have appeared in "Rays from the Red Cross." The spiritual approach to the basis of astrology, planets, signs, houses, and astrological influences on the arts are all discussed.

STUDY IN ZODIACAL SYMBOLOGY, Henry Van Stone. $2.95p 109pp. SYM74/ASA. Van Stone relates the meaning of the planetary and zodiacal sign symbols to Buddhist and Egyptian origins in this esoteric study.

STUDY OF ASTROLOGY, Henry Weingarten. $7.95p ISBN 0-88231-029-1, 176pp. ASI. This standard textbook is used in astrology schools and gives a simple and reliable method for horoscope interpretation. This presentation of the principles of astrological analysis from a modern viewpoint supplies exercises, a summary of important concepts and a suggested reading list.

SUN AND MOON POLARITY IN YOUR HOROSCOPE, Robert Hughes. $6.00p 176pp. AFA77. Delineations are given for the one hundred forty-four combinations of Sun and Moon signs. This approach facilitates the quick synthesis of a chart.

SUN-ASCENDANT RULERSHIPS: Their Influence in the Horoscopes, Esther V. Leinbach. $7.25p ISBN 0-914350-00-5, VUL73. This is a detailed analysis of the effects on the native's personality of the planetary rulers of the Sun sign and Ascendant in the individual natal chart.

SUN SIGNS, Linda Goodman. $3.50p ISBN 0-553-14695-5; $6.95c ISBN 0-553-01182-0, 488pp. BAN68. This is a basic introductory guide to Sun-sign astrology. SUN SIGNS is the most popular astrology book ever published. More than three million copies have been sold and the book has appeared on the New York Times Bestseller List.

SUN SIGN SUCCESS, Joseph Polansky. $2.25p INN. This astrological guide shows how success may be obtained for each of the twelve Sun signs.

SUPPLEMENT TO CAROLYN DODSON'S CARD READING FOR ASTROLOGERS, Sophia Mason. $4.00p 60pp. MAS. The author expands upon Dodson's book, giving explanations of the elements for every card and better understanding of the transits.

SYDNEY OMARR'S ASTROLOGICAL REVELATIONS ABOUT YOU, Sydney Omarr. $1.25p 239pp. NEW73. General analyses of Sun signs and approximate rising signs.

SYMBOLIC DIRECTIONS IN MODERN ASTROLOGY, Charles E.O. Carter, $3.00p 88pp. HEA.

SYNASTRY: The Art of Chart Comparison, Robert Carl Jansky. $9.00p 40pp. ASA74. These eight lessons on synastry teach the technique of comparing the planetary positions of two natal charts to determine compatibility. Using the reader's own chart in relation to others, Jansky shows how to identify compatibilities, problem areas and their resolutions.

SYNASTRY: Understanding Human Relations Through Astrology, Ronald Davison. $15.95c ISBN 0-88231-016-X, 352pp. ASI77. A comprehensive survey of the various techniques of horoscope comparison. The author has discovered "the relationship horoscope," an entirely new way of charting in a single horoscope the relationship between two people. He also introduces new methods of determining the quality of that relationship.

TABLES OF EVENTS, Reinhold Ebertin. $3.50p 48pp. HBV. These tables simplify rectification (the correction of birthtime when it is unknown), progressions and solar arc directions.

TAKING THE KID GLOVES OFF, Garth Allen. $3.25p 48pp. CLA75. This is a comprehensive in-depth evaluation of the meanings of the planets from a collection of essays that were originally printed in American Astrology Magazine.

TECHNIQUE OF PREDICTION, Ronald Davison. $7.00p ISBN 85243-172-4, 152pp. FOW55. This complete system of secondary directing (progressed and converse) is a new method of prediction combining the author's research and original findings with the Arabian system of secondary directions. Fully illustrated with copious examples from a number of selected horoscopes with special tables for the easy calculation of the minor measures.

TECHNIQUE OF RECTIFICATION, Charles Jayne. $6.00p 37pp. ASB72. Based on Jayne's twenty-five years of experience in astrology, this very technical work gives exact methods for rectification of a chart, primarily using solar Ascendant arc directions and vertical arcs.

TECHNIQUE OF SOLAR RETURNS, Alexandre Volguine. $15.95c ISBN 0-88231-011-9, 217pp. ASI76. Both beginners and experienced astrologers will be able to use this book. It teaches how to calculate a solar return, the relationship of the solar return to the natal chart, the meaning of the planets, signs, houses and aspects in the solar return, timing of events and more.

TERRESTRIAL ASTROLOGY, Stephen Skinner. $39.50c ISBN 0-7100-0553-9, 308pp. ROU80. Geomancy divination by Earth ranks alongside the Tarot, astrology and the I Ching as an important form of divination. This complete history covers its various manifestations in different cultures as well as being a practical manual showing how to cast and interpret geomantic figures. It also provides an examination of the relationship between astrology and geomancy.

THAT INCONJUNCT QUINCUNX, Frances Sakoian and Louis Acker. $2.50p 75pp. NES72. The quincunx, a seldom discussed and minor planetary aspect, is analyzed through the planets.

THE 360 DEGREES OF THE ZODIAC, Adriano Carelli. $4.50p 199pp. AFA51. The author gives a meditation for each zodiacal degree along with historical references.

TIME OUT OF MIND, Marc Robertson. $3.50p 46pp. AFA. Robertson examines the correlation between reincarnation and a natal chart.

TOPOCENTRIC SYSTEM, Vendel Polich. $15.00p 192pp. AFA75. The topocentric system of houses enables the astrologer to cut the zodiacal circle into twelve equal arcs. A table of houses and all oblique ascensions for latitudes are included.

TO RULE BOTH DAY AND NIGHT: Astrology in the Bible, Midrash and Talmud, Rabbi Joel C. Dobin. $11.95c ISBN 0-89281-000-9, 256pp. INT/WEI. The Bible, Midrash and Talmud are the richest sources of astrology existing in the Western tradition. The author, equipped with a knowledge of Hebrew, Aramaic and the Jewish wisdom traditions, has researched the astrology of the ancient Hebrews. Many theories and concepts are presented including the Kabbalistic balance of the planetary rulers.

TRADITIONAL SYMBOLISM IN ASTROLOGY AND THE CHARACTER TRAITS METHOD, Michel and Francoise Gauquelin. $5.00p 58pp. LAB80.

TRANSCENDENTAL ASTROLOGY, A.G.S. Norris. $9.95c 288pp. WEI30. First published in London in 1930, the material will interest students who wish to understand the more spiritual implications of the symbols of astrology. Tables and diagrams illustrate the Seven Worlds with planetary, numerical and alphabetical correspondences. The author discusses the Seven Vibrations of Harmony, the Lotus of the Threefold Soul, the origin of True Zodical Glyphs and more.

TRANSITS, Herbert Smith. $4.00p 42pp. AFA. An in-depth study of transiting planets written in Victorian style.

TRANSITS, Clara M. Darr. $10.75p 126pp. DAR71. This is a comprehensive look at transits giving guidelines for the six major aspects between each of the planets including the Sun and Moon. There are sections on Pluto, the Moon's nodes, eclipses and Fortuna.

TRANSIT AND PLANETARY PERIODS, Sepharial. $3.50p 94pp. WEI70. This book examines the length and continuity of transits with an explanation of apparant breaks in their action. Topics include new moons, conjunctions, planetary periods and mean motion.

TRANSITS INCONJUNCT, Frances Sakoian and Louis Acker. $3.50p 60pp. NES78. The authors give their interpretations of planets forming in an inconjunct (quincunx) aspect by transit.

TRANSITS IN PLAIN ENGLISH, Press and Ima Roberts. $6.45p ISBN 0-914350-11-0, 120pp. VUL75. This first book in the "Plain English" series is an unesoteric approach to daily planetary transits. A list of keywords is given for each planet, followed by an analysis of planetary transits and aspects. Transits of the full and new Moon, the nodes and the Part of Fortune are also included.

TRANSITS OF JUPITER, Frances Sakoian and Louis Acker. $3.00p 72pp. NES74. One of a series of pamphlets on planetary transits, in which the authors analyze the transits of each planet through the houses and then as it comes into a major aspect with each of the other planets.

TRANSITS OF MARS, Frances Sakoian and Louis Acker. $3.00p 55pp. NES74.

TRANSITS OF MERCURY, Frances Sakoian and Louis Acker. $3.00p 80pp. NES75.

TRANSITS OF NEPTUNE, Frances Sakoian and Louis Acker. $3.00p 78pp. NES72.

TRANSITS OF PLUTO, Frances Sakoian and Louis Acker. $3.00p 64pp. NES72.

TRANSITS OF SATURN, Marc Robertson. $5.00c 73pp. ACN73. Robertson suggests ways to deal with Saturn transits by sign, quadrant, house or aspect.

TRANSITS OF THE MOON, Frances Sakoian and Louis Acker. $3.00p 60pp. NES75.

TRANSITS OF THE SUN, Frances Sakoian and Louis Acker. $3.00p 67pp. NES75.

TRANSITS OF URANUS, Frances Sakoian and Louis Acker. $3.00p 78pp. NES73.

TRANSITS OF VENUS, Frances Sakoian and Louis Acker. $3.00p 72pp. NES75.

TRANSITS SIMPLIFIED, Frances Sakoian and Louis Acker. $10.95p 227pp. NES76. This volume is based on the authors' previously published series of pamphlets giving delineations of planetary transits. This edition is in summary outline form, using keywords to describe the planetary transits.

TRANSITS: The Time of Your Life, Betty Lundsted. $6.95p ISBN 0-87728-503-9, 176pp. WEI80. An innovative approach to using transits for personal growth and development. This second book by the author of ASTROLOGICAL INSIGHTS INTO PERSONALITY is drawn from her background in both psychology and metaphysics and is directed toward helping readers through life's recurring cycles.

TRANSITS: THE NEXT STEP IN OUR BECOMING, Tracy Marks. $4.00p 43pp. SAG. These five essays on the outer planetary transits focus on developing the right attitude toward transits, interpreting transits, learning from the past, preparing for the future and responding constructively to transits of the five outer planets. Worksheets and examples are included.

TRANSNEPTUNE-EPHEMERIDE: 1890-2000, Ruth Brummund. $14.50p 209pp. AFA72. Positions of the trans-Neptunian planets are given for every ten days.

TRANSPLUTO, John Robert Hawkins. $9.00p 132pp. HAW76. Bacchus (Transpluto), says Hawkins, is not a Uranian planet; there is solid astronomical evidence that it exists. The author relates the myth of Bacchus (Dionysus), the Greek god, to the characteristics of Transpluto, the planet. Final chapters delineate the planet through the signs, houses, aspects and midpoints. The book includes a Transpluto ephemeris from 1750 to 2100, compiled and programmed by Neil Michelsen.

ASTROLOGY INSIDE OUT

Bruce Nevin

This is an excellent introduction to astrology and much more. Its theoretical framework, integrating esoteric tradition with modern harmonic research in astrology and recent developments in physics and psychology, will interest every astrological reader. Through its many ingenious visualization and meditation exercises, even seasoned astrologers will learn new ways to recognize and interpret astrological patterning from the 'inside out.'

In Part One, even before looking at a horoscope, the reader learns to translate the events and circumstances of life into the symbol-language of astrology. The circle of houses and its contents become vivid realities as tools for interpreting experience, solving problems and resolving conflicts.

In Part Two, rather than merely telling the reader what the horoscope means from the 'outside in,' the inside knowledge gained in Part One is applied in even greater depth to the art of horoscope delineation. For example, by identifying the contribution of each sign's ruler, exaltation, detriment and fall in a unique analytical format, sources of strength and difficulty are identified in the horoscope.

Now everyone can learn, teach, and practice astrology from the inside out. 300 pages, paperback, $9.95

Available at your local bookstore by July 1981

TRIPTYCH, Dane Rudhyar. $8.95p ISBN 0-88231-036-4, 320pp. ASI68. Rudhyar extracts from traditional astrology a great wealth of psychological and spiritual meaning. Interpretations of the zodiacal signs, the houses and the planets are presented in inspiring language.

TRUE HOROSCOPE OF THE U.S., Helen M. Boyd. $7.25p ISBN 0-88231-007-0, 180pp. ASI75. The author uses one hundred charts and the records of the Continental Congress to support her thesis that the true date of the birth of the United States was July 6, 1775 at 11:00 AM, L.M.T. in Philadelphia, Pennsylvania. She also includes the charts of alternative birthtimes advanced by other astrologers and dates of significant historical events.

TRUTH ABOUT ASTROLOGY, Sydney Omarr. $1.00p AFA.

TURNING OPPOSITIONS INTO CONJUNCTIONS: Gestalt Therapy and Astrology, Tracy Marks. $2.00p ISBN 0-933620-05-5, 28pp. SAG. The theory and dialoging techniques of gestalt therapy and their relationship to the lunar cycle are explored. Also discussed is the use of gestalt therapy with the birthchart, techniques for constructive chart interpretation and sample dialogues expressive of Mars/Venus and Sun/Moon conflicts.

TURN OF A LIFETIME ASTROLOGICALLY, Ivy M. Goldstein-Jacobson. $9.00 115pp. GOJ64. This book gives a simplified method for calculating primary arcs which can be used to pinpoint event dates to the exact year, month and almost always to the exact day. It includes all the necessary tables in larger print than usual. Magazine size, bound in heavy paper (not paperback).

TWELFTH HOUSE, Tracy Marks. $4.00p ISBN 0-933620-02-0, 88pp. SAG78. Mark's in-depth study of all the psychological and spiritual meanings of the twelfth house gives detailed interpretations of the planets, lunar nodes and several twelfth-house profiles, with worksheets for interpreting one's own twelfth-house energies. It also includes"And Then The Chart Spoke," an illuminating poem about the "answers" that may not be discovered in the astrological chart.

TWELVE DOORS TO THE SOUL, Jane Evans. $4.75p ISBN 0-8356-0521-3, 205pp. THE79. The author presents an astrology of the inner self which incorporates the concepts of a reincarnating ego. She explores clues to past lives which can be found in the zodiac.

TWENTIETH CENTURY TABLE OF HOUSES, A. LeRoi Simmons. $6.00c ISBN 0-9605126-2-4 202pp. AQB73. This modern table of houses uses the Placidean system and gives a simplified arrangement of the latitudes of the signs and the sidereal time at five minute intervals. Large easy to read print.

2001: THE PENFIELD COLLECTION, Marc Penfield. $9.95p ISBN 0-914350-16-1, VUL78. This reference text gives birth data of famous people from all ages. In his preface Penfield explains how he conducted his research, what sources he contacted, the changeover from the Gregorian calendar and the dates various countries in the world adopted standard time.

UNDERSTANDING PLANETARY PLACEMENTS, Sophia Mason. $4.00p 65pp. MAS. The author stresses the importance of understanding the correlation between planets, signs and houses and how they affect our emotions.

UNITED STATE'S WHEEL OF DESTINY, Diana Stone. $4.50p 131pp. AFA76. An esoteric, mundane astrological approach is used in this subjective interpretation of United States history.

UNKNOWN PLANETS, Charles Jayne. $6.00p 53pp. ASB74. This discussion of the unknown planets is accompanied by an ephemerides of Pan, Isis, Morya, Hermes, Osiris, Midas and Lion plus a ninety-year ephemeris of Sigma for every ten days.

URANIAN ASTROLOGY GUIDE, Sylvia Sherman and Jori Frank. $14.95c ISBN 75-38487, 200pp. AMS76. The book explains how to chart a Uranian or trans-Neptunian chart. An ephemeris by Neil Michelsen is also included.

URANUS, ESOTERIC AND MUNDANE, John Townley. $4.95p WEI. A comprehensive discussion of the effect of Uranus in myth, religion, science, self-understanding, the bizarre, sexual perversion, revolution, war and the esoteric. The author includes some interpretation of Uranus in the signs and houses in the personal chart.

URANUS IN TRANSIT, Clara M. Darr. $3.75p 48pp. DAR76. This work takes Uranus through the houses and gives the major aspects.

URANUS-NEPTUNE-PLUTO: The Spiritual Trinity, Ted George. $12.00c ISBN 0-932782-01-9, 225pp. ART. Natal, mundane, spiritual and karmic delineations are given for each member of this powerful trio through the signs and houses and in aspect to all the other planets, including Vulcan (Chiron) and Persephone.

VENUS, THE GIFT OF LOVE, Martin Schulman. $7.95p 150pp. GLB. Schulman reaches into the secrets of the ancients to reveal an astrological approach to the beauty of love. The book provides a discussion of Venus through each sign and house, delineation of several horoscopes of famous people and a self-contained Venus Ephemeris.

VOCATIONAL GUIDANCE BY ASTROLOGY, Charles E. Luntz. $4.95p ISBN 0-87542-435-X, 213pp. LLE78. Luntz furnishes all the tools and rules needed for using astrology to help an individual locate a suitable and creative vocation. The author's lifelong experience in the business world and his understanding of human relations and career motivations is the reason for the success of this method in large corporations. The system identifies the individual's most satisfying and appropriate vocation.

WAY OF ASTROLOGY, Ivy M. Goldstein-Jacobson. $11.00c 233pp. GOJ67. This is primarily a history of astrology and the development of the natal chart. It also describes how to read the natal chart forecast with progressions and avoid misfortune and danger through election charts. A dictionary of terms is included.

WHAT'S A DIURNAL?, Maxine Taylor. $4.50p 51pp. TAY76. The diurnal chart uses the natal, progressed and transiting planets for predicting events. Detailed instructions for casting the diurnal chart are given plus twenty-six examples including the diurnals of Patricia Hearst.

WHAT'S A RELOCATED CHART?, Maxine Taylor. $2.00p 11pp. TAY76. A natal chart can be relocated every time the native changes residence. This pamphlet explains how to cast a relocation chart and interpret it. Three sample charts and interpretations illustrate the text.

WHAT'S MY SIGN, Mary Orser and Rick and Glory Brightfield. $1.95p ISBN 0-06-080434-3, HAR78.

WHAT'S WRONG WITH YOUR SUN SIGN?, Barbara Watters. $4.50p 293pp. AFA70. This is a revealing analysis of the weaknesses and peculiarities in each of the twelve Sun signs.

WHAT YOUR ASTROLOGER NEVER TOLD YOU, Maxine Taylor. $4.00p 48pp. TAY. This funny, tongue-in-cheek book on the twelve Sun signs is written for the staunch, astrological skeptic.

WHEN YOUR SUN RETURNS, Jinni Meyer and Joanne Wickenburg. $3.95p SEA. The solar return chart symbolizes the kinds of experiences that will unfold in the year ahead. This teacher's manual and text for advanced students psychologically approaches the techniques of interpreting the soli-lunar returns, tailored specifically to Tropical Astrology.

WHY WERE YOU BORN, Olson and Hanratty. $6.95p AFA.

WITNESS OF THE STARS, Rev. E.W. Bullinger, $5.00 facsimile reprint (1893) 204pp. HEA. Bullinger presents the facts related in 850 A.D. by Albumazer, the Arab astronomer, to the Califphs of Grenada and the tables drawn up to Ulugh Bleigh, the Tartar prince and astronomer, about 1450 A.D., who documents Arabian astronomy as it has come down from earliest times. The author includes scores of footnotes and two folded maps. The print is large and easy to read.

WOMAN'S ASTROLOGY: The Woman's Astrological Guide to a Future Worth Having, Tiffany Holmes. $5.95p ISBN 0-525-23597-3; $9.95c ISBN 0-525-04775-1, EPD77. Tiffany Holmes says "The product of my research is so arranged to show that the positive connotations generally went to the male while the negative side tended to be alloted to the female. My own contention is that both sexes are capable of various manifestations of a sign, and whether behavior reflects favorably on the individual will depend on both the harmony of aspects to the sign(s) in question in the natal chart and the individual's personal standards."

WORLD HOROSCOPE: Hebrew Astrology, Sepharial. $3.75p ISBN 0-572-00243-2, 70pp. WFO65. Sepharial identifies biblical references indicating the influence of the stars and suggests a key to studying scriptural prophecy. He gives an interpretation of the world horoscope on which all international prediction is based.

WRITING FOR THE U.S. ASTROLOGY MARKET, Carole Veta. $4.95p ISBN 0-930840-09-7, 67pp. NIN79. 1980-1981 edition. Published every two years, this comprehensive guide to the astrology market for free lance writers includes complete how-to information on manuscript submission and current editorial needs. It includes three catagories: non-paying magazines, paying magazines and book publishers.

X-MARKS MY PLACE, Paul Councel. $4.25p 78pp. DAR38. The author discusses location astrology and explains where to relocate by using the provided location maps and astro-geographic tables in conjunction with the natal chart and progressions.

YEARS AHEAD: A Prophetic Astrological Odyssey Into the Future, Robert B. Shannon. $15.99c PHP80. This book explores the future to the year 3797 AD, and through predictive mundane astrology provides an astounding look at the important conditions, trends and events that will shape human destiny in the future. Shannon describes dated events such as a new global economy emerging out of worldwide economic collapse, the beginning and outcome of World War III, a new Golden Age of peace and prosperity and much more.

YOD AND OTHER POINTS IN YOUR HOROSCOPE, Helen Paul and Bridget Mary O'Toole. $5.55p ISBN 0-914350-7-X, 52pp. VUL77. This text analyzes many infrequently discussed points including the little known Yod aspect-pattern. It also covers midpoints, Solstice Points, Vertex, Composite Points, planetary nodes and Decision Points. Brief and to the point, it is illustrated with many examples.

YOUR BEST PLACE: Astrological Relocation Techniques, David Warren. $4.95p ISBN 0-930840-06-2, 40pp. NIN77. This is a comprehensive treatment of a variey of relocation techniques including interpretations and example charts.

YOUR CHILD'S HOROSCOPE, Max Heindel and Augusta Foss Heindel. $1.50p 100pp. ROS73. Volumes 1 and 2. A variety of children's charts and case studies are used to illustrate how to interpret a child's horoscope.

YOUR COSMIC MIRROR, Jinni Meyer and Joanne Wickenburg. $1.50p SEA. This supplemental workbook has been prepared to help the student organize the large amount of information available in the SPIRAL OF LIFE. It provides key phrases, condensed to the central core meaning of the houses, signs and planets, to be used in interpreting a chart in written form.

YOUR DESTINY IN THE ZODIAC AND ITS MASTERY, Louise B. Brownell. $2.50p HEA.

YOUR MOTIVE FACTOR, Olson and Hanratty. $3.50p AFA.

YOUR SUN'S RETURN, Alfa Lindanger. $2.50p 47pp. MAC78. This exposition of the technique of computing a solar return chart includes thirteen chart illustrations, the noon date method of finding an unknown birthtime, and an accurate method of rectification by arcs of events, aspects, horoscopal houses, Part of Fate, intercepted signs and table of right ascensions. A suitable book for beginners as well as for professional astrologers.

ZODIAC, A LIFE EPITOME, Walter Sampson. $15.95c ISBN 0-88231-019-4, 420pp. ASI26. The esoteric aspects of astrology are emphasized in this classic work. The inner meanings of the signs of the zodiac are interpreted through the teachings of Christianity, the ancient mystery teachings and modern anthropological and psychological theories.

ZODIACAL SYMBOLOGY AND ITS PLANETARY POWER, Isidore Kozminsky. $5.00p 194pp. AFA. This volume gives delineations for the planets through the degrees of each of the twelve signs.

ZODIAC AND THE SALTS OF SALVATION, Inez E. Perry and George Carey. $13.95c 352pp. WEI71. This is an esoteric analysis and synthesis of the relation of the mineral salts in body chemistry to the signs of the zodiac. These salts are used in homeopathy.

ZODIAC AND THE SOUL, Charles E.O. Carter. $7.50c ISBN 0-8356-5098-7, 120pp. THE28. Some deeper philosophical aspects of astrology are discussed in this inspiring metaphysical work.

ZODIAC AS A KEY TO HISTORY, Zipporah P. Dobyns. $4.00p 23pp. TIA68. Dobyns presents her theory on astrological ages and sub-age divisions to explain the confusion over the timing of the Aquarian Age and to better understand present day trends.

ZODIAC COLORING BOOK, Dr. Diane Lerner. $2.50p ISBN 0-914350-24-2, VUL77. This astrological coloring book, for children of all ages, shows the twelve signs and their rulers.

ZODIAC WITHIN EACH SIGN: A Study of the Duads and the Decanates, Frances Sakoian and Louis Acker. $5.95p 142pp. NES75. The decanates and duads of each of the twelve signs are examined and explained with the aid of some charts.

3

Ephemerides

AMERICAN EPHEMERIS FOR THE 20TH CENTURY 1900-2000, Neil F. Michelsen. $15.95p (Midnight) ISBN 0-917086-19-8; (Noon) 0-917086-20-1, 608 pp. AST80. In addition to one hundred one years of planetary positions all in one comprehensive ephemeris, this book also contains: Sun and Moon longitudes to 1 second, the planets to .1 minute calculated for GMT; Solar and lunar eclipses; aspectarian of Jupiter through Pluto; Chiron's position; the Moon's mean Node as well as true node and much more.

AMERICAN EPHEMERIS 1901 TO 1930, Neil F. Michelsen. $14.95p ISBN 0-917086-12-0, AST77.

AMERICAN EPHEMERIS 1931 to 1940, Neil F. Michelsen. $5.00p ISBN 0-917086-07-4, AST76.

AMERICAN EPHEMERIS 1931 TO 1980 & BOOK OF TABLES, Neil F. Michelsen. $25.00c ISBN 0-917086-01-5, 728pp. AST76. An ephemeris is the required tool of the practicing astrologer. These ephemerides, which are also suitable for beginners, provide: daily midnight Sun longitude; daily midnight and noon Moon longitude (to the nearest second of arc); daily planetary longitudes, latitudes and declinations to the nearest minute of arc; Moon phenomena and a complete aspectarian.

AMERICAN EPHEMERIS 1941 to 1950, Neil F. Michelsen. $5.00p ISBN 0-917086-05-8, AST76.

AMERICAN EPHEMERIS 1951 TO 1960, Neil F. Michelsen. $5.00p ISBN 0-917086-04-4, AST76.

AMERICAN EPHEMERIS 1961 TO 1970, Neil F. Michelsen. $5.00p ISBN 0-917086-06-6, AST76.

AMERICAN EPHEMERIS 1971 TO 1980, Neil F. Michelsen. $5.00p ISBN 0-917086-02-3, AST76.

AMERICAN EPHEMERIS 1981, Neil F. Michelsen. $1.00p ISBN 0-917086-24-4, AST80.

AMERICAN EPHEMERIS 1981 TO 1990, Neil F. Michelsen. $5.00p ISBN 0-917086-10-4, AST77.

AMERICAN EPHEMERIS 1991 TO 2000, Neil F. Michelsen. $5.00p ISBN 0-917086-21-4, AST80.

AMERICAN SIDEREAL EPHEMERIS 1976-2000, Neil F. Michelsen. $20.00p ISBN 0-917086-33-3, 320pp. AST81. This is the first in a projected series of four volumes covering the entire twentieth century. It includes longitude and declination to a second of arc, right ascension in hours, minutes and seconds for all planets and much more. The introduction and instructions are by James Eshelman.

ASTEROID EPHEMERIS, Zipporah P. Dobyns. $15.00p TIA77. This ephemeris gives the daily positions and delineations for Ceres, Pallas, Juno and Vesta during the years 1883-1999. Dobyns' introduction offers a discussion of philosophical issues, astronomical information, mythological background and psychological principles associated with asteroids. Calculated and computer programmed by Neil Michelsen and Rique Pottenger.

ASTRO-GRAPHIC SIDEREAL EPHEMERIS 1981-1985, $5.00p 32pp. AGR81. Designed and executed by Robert Hand, this sidereal ephemeris presents two months per page in five year volumes. 1981-1985 is available now and subsequent volumes will follow.

ASTROLOGER'S EPHEMERIDES, Aries Press. $3.00c 1890-1900, 1900-1910; $2.00p 1880-1890, 1890-1900, 1900-1910, 1910-1920, ARI. These ten-year volumes are purse-pocket size and calculated for noon Greenwich. $3.00c 1930-1940; $2.00p 1930-1940. Calculated for midnight Greenwich.

ASTROLOGICAL EPHEMERIS FOR 1981, $2.00p ISBN 0-935146-54-7, MOR. This ephemeris contains the daily planetary, stellar and lunar movements in one easy-to-carry volume. Also included are the daily Moon positions for all United States time zones.

COMPLETE PLANETARY EPHEMERIS, Hieratic Publishing. $17.00p ISBN 0-915820-10-2; $25.00c ISBN 0-915820-00-5, 616pp. HIE75. Midnight ephemeris covering the years 1950 to 2000 including true longitude, latitudes, right ascension and declination.

CONCISE PLANETARY EPHEMERIS 1900-1950, Hieratic Publishing. $10.00p ISBN 0-915820-06-4; $17.00c ISBN 0-915820-05-6, HIE79. These accurately computed and conveniently bound ephemerides are available in fifty year periods covering the twentieth century.

CONCISE PLANETARY EPHEMERIS 1900-1950 NOON, Hieratic Publishing. $10.00p ISBN 0-915820-08-0; $17.00c ISBN 0-915820-07-2, HIE79.

CONCISE PLANETARY EPHEMERIS 1950-2000, Hieratic Publishing. $10.00p ISBN 0-915820-02-1; $17.00c ISBN 0-915820-01-3, HIE77.

CONCISE PLANETARY EPHEMERIS 1950-2000 NOON, Hieratic Publishing. $10.00p ISBN 0-915820-04-8; $17.00c ISBN 0-915820-03-4, HIE78.

DIE DEUTSCHE EPHEMERIDE, Vol 1: 1850-1889 $26.00c; Vol 2: 1890-1930 $26.50c; Vol 3: 1931-1950 $24.50c; Vol 4: 1951-1,0 $20.00c; Vol 5: 1/1-1970 $20.00c; Vol 6: 1971-1980 $20.00c; Vol 7: 1981-2000 $23.50c HBV. This compact, accurate set of ephemerides provides the daily sidereal time and positions of the Sun to the seconds of arc. It includes tables of diurnal proportional logarithms and daily positions for Pluto given from 1/1. It is calculated for Greenwich noon up to 1930 and for Greenwich midnight from 1931 through 2000.

EPHEMERIS OF THE GREAT COMETS, Carl Ramus. $2.75p AFA. The years 1402 through 1948 are covered.

EPHEMERIS OF THE MOON: 1800-2000, Hugh MacCraig. $6.75c 247pp. MAC75. Even in this computer age, the mathematical calculations in this book are noteworthy. Computed for Greenwich noon, it contains date and time of Moon's entry into each sign, new Moon, full Moon, solar ingresses, major conjunction, and Easter date table. Zodiacal longitude calculations are reduced to a minimum.

EPHEMERIS 1890-1950, A. LeRoi Simmons. $17.00c ISBN 0-05126-0-8, 407pp. AQB70. Simmons' ephemeris gives the daily positions for the planets and the Moon's nodes over a sixty-one year period, computed for noon GMT. Pluto's positions are given every eight days, and latitudes and longitudes are provided for major cities in the United States including Hawaii. It has large, easy-to-read logarithm tables, and is considered quite accurate.

EPHEMERIS 1950-1975, A. LeRoi Simmons. $14.00c ISBN 0-9605126-1-6, 375pp. AQB77. This ephemeris picks up in 1950 where the author left off in his previously published ephemeris. It also includes the longitudes and latitudes of the major United States cities including Hawaii, large print logarithm tables with instructions, a completely detailed method for horoscope erection with examples and a map showing the latest time zone changes.

GOLGGE EPHEMERIDES, $9.00p 132pp. HBV. 1961-65, 1966-70, 1971-75, 1976-80, 1981-85. Longitude, latitude and declinations are given for midnight Greenwich Time for the Sun, Moon and planets, including Pluto. Positions for the Sun and Moon are accurate to the nearest second of arc, and noon positions for the Moon are given for greater accuracy. It includes a complete daily aspectarian and lists geographical coordinates of major cities throughout the world.

GRAPHIC EPHEMERIS 1980, 1981, 1982, 1983, 1984, Robert Hand. $5.00 each, AGR80.

ISIS/OSIRIS EPHEMERIS, $5.00p ISBN 0-935146-02-4, 112pp. MOR. The esoteric suns, Isis and Osiris, are charted for the years 1900 to 2000. These suns highlight spiritual awakening and growth in the natal chart.

PLUTO EPHEMERIS, Omega Associates. $5.00p OMA. This ephemeris is calculated for midnight Greenwich and gives the declination, longitude and latitude in ten-day intervals for the years 1771 to 2000.

PLUTO EPHEMERIS 1900-2000, Lynne Palmer. $10.00p AFA74. Contains daily geocentric longitude and declination of the planet for the years 1900-2000.

PLUTO-TABELLE 1851-2000, Reinhold Ebertin. $3.00p 24pp. HBV75. Pluto positions for the first of every month and interpolation tables for daily movements.

RAPHAEL'S EPHEMERIS, Raphael. $3.50p WFO. This annual publication gives the longitudes of the planets, sidereal time for noon each day of the year. Copies are available for any one year from 1860 to date.

SIMPLIFIED SCIENTIFIC EPHEMERIS, Rosicrucian Fellowship, single years, $1.50; decade volumes, $9.00, ROS. Calculated for Greenwich noon, these standard ephemerides are available from 1900 in single year pamphlets or bound together in 10 year periods up to 1999.

SUN IS SHINING: HELIO 1653-2050, Michael Erlewine. $5.00p AFA75. Erlewine has developed a systematic approach for constructing heliocentric charts which exclude the Moon, Ascendant, Descendant, Midheaven, houses and signs of the zodiac. This simplified system uses the Sun as the center of the chart and complements the traditional geocentric Earth centered chart.

200 YEAR EPHEMERIS, Hugh MacCraig. $15.00c 420pp. MAC47. Although not an ephemeris for calculating an accurate chart, this book gives planetary positions for the first day of each month from 1800-2000. It includes declinations, latitudes, direct and retrograde stations and solar and lunar eclipses. It also gives longitudes and latitudes for seven thousand cities of the world.

TWO YEAR MIDPOINT EPHEMERIS FOR 1980-1981, $5.00s ASB. This is the only ephemeris on midpoints available.

4

Tables and Atlases

AFA TABLES OF HOUSES: Campanus, Koch or Placidus System, Astro Numeric Service. $12.00c each 178pp. AFA77. These three books each contain computer derived tables of latitudes from zero to sixty-six degrees and list all of the cusps to one-tenth of a minute of arc.

AMERICAN ATLAS, Neil F. Michelsen. $19.50c ISBN 0-917086-16-3, AST78.

AMERICAN BOOK OF TABLES, Neil F. Michelsen. $6.00p ISBN 0-917086-03-1, AST76.

ARIES PRESS TABLE OF HOUSES, Aries Press. $4.50p ISBN 0-933646-00-3, 156pp. ARI. These tables are calculated for major cities throughout the world from the equator to sixty-six degrees latitude. Instructions for calculating southern latitude charts are included.

ASCENDANT TABLES, Spenceley. $2.00p 24pp. MAC75. These tables give the sign and degree rising for each hour of every fourth day for all places in the vicinity of 41 degrees N. Instructions on how to make a horoscope and description of Zodiacal types are also included. A fine little book for setting up a chart quickly without detailed mathematical calculations.

ASTROLOGER'S ASTRONOMICAL HANDBOOK, Jeff Mayo. $3.75p ISBN 85243-058-2, 126pp. FOW65. This reference work provides the student and practicing astrologer with a guide to a clearer understanding of the elements of astrological theory and charting.

ASTROLOGICAL ATLAS OF THE UNITED STATES, Astro Numeric Service. $15.00c 321pp. AFA76. This atlas features the longitudes and latitudes for more than thirty thousand cities in the United States. Although maps are not included, tables, instructions and time conversions are given.

BIRTHPLACE TABLES OF HOUSES, Walter Koch and Elizabeth Schaeck. $7.95p ISBN 0-88231-021-6; $10.50c ISBN 0-88231-020-8, 184pp. ASI77. Many of the world's leading professional astrologers have abandoned the old Placidus, Regimontanus and Campanus systems for the new "birthplace" system. The mathematical accuracy of these intermediate cusps provide material for interpretation. For northern latitudes 0-66 degrees and a table of Ascendants 66-75 degrees latitude.

CALCULATOR KEY TO ASTROLOGY, Juliann. $4.00p ISBN 0-933646-02-X, 64pp. ARI77. Simple step-by-step instructions on the use of a four-function calculator in preparing natal charts, solar returns, double interpolation for house cusps, aspects, midpoints and secondary progressions.

COMPLETE ASTRO-MEDICAL INDEX, Joan M. Harmon. $7.50p 96pp. ASA. This work lists medical conditions likely to be associated with each planet by house, sign and aspect and includes a discussion of the Parts of Peril and Sickness.

COMPUTING HOROSCOPES WITH YOUR ELECTRONIC CALCULATOR, C.J. Puotinen. $5.95p ISBN 0-930840-07-0, 50pp. NIN78. A complete guide for using any calculator to interpolate from ephemerides or tables of houses. Instructions are given for computing house cusps to the minute. It also includes planetary correction by declination and longitude, solar arc progressions, second progressions, solar and lunar returns, biorhythms and midpoints.

DALTON'S TABLES OF HOUSES, Joseph Dalton. $8.95c 80pp. MAC76. Intermediate cusps are given to the nearest tenth of a degree, the MC is calculated to an exact even degree to aid in interpolation and the Ascendant is calculated to an exact even degree of latitude. End columns are repeated so no page flipping is necessary, and there is eye-saving large type on 11 x 7½" pages. Each degree of latitude from twenty-two to sixty degrees North is given with full instructions for calculating latitudes from the Equator to twenty-one degrees.

EASY TABLES WITH EXAMPLES, J. Allen Jones. $4.00p ISBN 0-912368-16-0, 38pp. GOL. These examples include patterns for setting up charts for north latitudes (west and east) and south latitudes (west and east) using a noon or midnight ephemeris.

ECLIPSES 1865-2000, George Hardsil. $2.50p 22pp. AFA. The author discusses the interactive effects of eclipses on politics and earthquakes. Tables are also included for universal and sidereal times 1865 through 2000.

50 THOUSAND BIRTHDAYS, Paul Field. $2.25p 72pp. MAC. Fifty thousand birthdays and more in this compilation. Eight graphs have been charted showing the months prominent persons from various professions were born including eight thousand from WHO'S WHO. Fifteen charts give the names and birthdates by month of notable persons. Listing by each month gives the name, date and place of birth of artists.

FOWLER'S COMPENDIUM OF NATIVITIES, Jadwiga M. Harrison. $14.95p ISBN 85243-360-3, 339pp. FOW80. Composed of five hundred concise biographies with the natal data necessary for the erection of charts. All sources are quoted and scrupulously checked.

GEOCENTRIC LONGITUDES AND DECLINATIONS, Raphael. $1.35p ISBN 0-572-00250-5, 35pp. WFO. Neptune, Herschel, Saturn, Jupiter and Mars are all included for the first of each month from 1900 to 2001.

LONGITUDES AND LATITUDES IN THE U.S., Eugene Derney. $6.00c AFA. Gives local Mean Time variations from Standard Time Greenwich Mean Time for more than twenty-five hundred cities in the United States.

LONGITUDES AND LATITUDES THROUGHOUT THE WORLD, Eugene Derney. $6.00c 134pp. AFA48. These tables give the LMT differences from Standard Time and Greenwich Mean Time for more than five thousand cities and towns in one hundred eighty-five countries.

RAPHAEL'S TABLE OF HOUSES FOR GREAT BRITAIN, Raphael. $1.40p WFO. These tables are serviceable not only for Great Britain but for all places in or near the latitude.

RAPHAEL'S TABLES OF HOUSES FOR NORTHERN LATITUDES, Raphael. $2.50p ISBN 0-572-00251-3, WFO. These tables embrace the whole of India and the United States. They include latitudes from the equator to 50 degrees north, and for Leningrad, 59 degrees 56 minutes north.

SOLAR ARC TABLES, Arthur Kickbusch. $2.35p AFA.

STUDENTS LARGE LOGARITHM TABLE, Aquarian Book Pub. $.75 AQB. 8 1/2" x 11". The table is mounted on cardboard, with detailed instructions for finding a logarithm. On the reverse side is a step-by-step method for erecting an accurate horoscope.

TABLE OF ASPECTS, Laurel Lowell. $4.75p 96pp. AFA. Lowell explains why aspects are important and describes their nature as well as covering the nodes, parallels, eclipses and decanates.

TABLE OF HOUSES, Wilhelm Koch. $13.00p 192pp. HBV. Birth locations are given from 0 to 60 degrees northern latitude with an ecliptic angle of 23 degrees 27 minutes.

TABLE OF HOUSES FOR U.S. LATITUDES, Magnus Jensen. $1.50 abridged HEA. This table of houses is part of the essential equipment needed to cast charts. Four pages of "The Song of the Spheres" are appended.

TABLE OF HOUSES, LATITUDE 1-66, $5.50p 313pp. ROS49. The Rosicrucians' original method is fully explained for use with these tables of North and South latitudes. They show the longitude and latitude of the United States and many foreign countries.

TABLES OF DIURNAL PLANETARY MOTION, Arthur D. Libin. $4.25p ISBN 0-88231-025-9, 186pp. ASI75. These computer-programmed tables can be used for calculating the Sun's apparant motion for every minute in the day, the range of diurnal motion for the planets and Moon and more accurate calculations when the Moon is shown for seconds of arc.

TABLES OF DIURNAL PLANETARY MOTION, American Federation of Astrologers. $4.25p AFA. Use of these tables enables a speedy determination of the proportional motion of any celestial body in longitude or right ascension for every minute of the day without logarithms.

TABLES OF DIURNAL PLANETARY MOTION, Ernest Grant. $5.00p 165pp. ASI. This tool teaches how to calculate the exact planetary positions at birth without the use of logarithms.

TABLES OF MIDHEAVENS AND ASCENDANTS, Ernest Grant. $5.50p AFA. These tables list forty-one thousand calculations of the Midheaven and Ascendant with Sidereal Time for each hour of local mean time every third day.

TIME CHANGES IN CANADA AND MEXICO, Doris Chase Doane. $7.00s 75pp. AFA68.

TIME CHANGES IN THE USA, Doris Chase Doane. $10.00s 191pp. AFA73. Calendars, Standard time, World Time, reference tables and the Uniform Time Act of 1966 are all included.

TIME CHANGES IN THE WORLD, Doris Chase Doane. $8.00s 101pp. AFA71.

TRUE LUNAR NODES: 1850-2000, Digicomp Research Corporation. $4.95p 160pp. DIG75. This book gives true (not average) positions of the Moon's nodes daily for midnight Greenwich time, covering the years 1850-2000. The accurate motion is necessary for accurate Sabian Symbol readings, aspects and progressions. The tables have been prepared with the aid of mathematical formulae supplied by the U.S. Naval Observatory.

5

Dictionary

AN ASTROLOGICAL WHO'S WHO, Marc Penfield. $10.00c ISBN 0-912240-08-3, 543pp. ARN72. This book contains five hundred charts and enables the student to evaluate astrological principles by applying them to the lives of well-known personalities.

ANNUAL DIAGRAM, Reinhold Ebertin. $8.00p 152pp. HBV73. Ebertin's book deals in particular with the graphic 45 degree ephemerides and serves as an introduction to their systematic and comprehensive application. These ephemerides are used to set up an annual diagram which gives the astrologer an easy-to-comprehend projected picture of the whole year. It also permits the astrologer to know when positive or negative reaction points appear.

A SHORT DICTIONARY OF ASTROLOGY, Marylee Bytheriver. $2.95p ISBN 0-06-090629-4, HAR78. This handbook explains all the obscure astrological terms encountered while learning and working with astrology.

ASTROLOGICAL DICTIONARY, L. Edward Johndro. $2.00p 41pp. AFA. This book includes keywords for each of the planets and information on aspects.

ASTROLOGICAL KEYWORDS, Manly Palmer Hall. $3.95p ISBN 0-8226-0299-7, 229pp. LIT75; $6.95c ISBN 0-89314-503-3, 229pp. PHR68. The keyword system is an efficient means by which the implications of a horoscope can be quickly analyzed with genuine understanding. This book is divided into over one hundred sections, each summarizing the basic interpretations of the various factors and elements.

ASTROLOGY BOOKS IN PRINT, Para Research Editorial Staff. $3.95p ISBN 0-914918-25-7, 128pp. PAR81. A comprehensive annotated listing of all astrological books available to the public. Includes projected publications from major publishers through 1982.

COMPLETE DICTIONARY OF ASTROLOGY, Alan Leo. $6.95p ISBN 0-89281-182-X, 216pp. INT/WEI29. This reference work defines technical terms and philosophical concepts with simple explanations. It was completed posthumously by Vivian Robson, acting as Leo's literary executor. Some of the entries are quite lengthy, making quick references difficult.

DAILY USE OF THE EPHEMERIS, Elizabeth Aldrich. $5.25p 67pp. HUG71. This short book gives the beginning astrologer full instructions for using an ephemeris accurately and with confidence.

DICTIONARY OF ASTROLOGY, James Wilson. $15.00c 406pp. WEI. First published in 1880, this classic text is of special interest to those interested in exploring old texts and manuscripts. Definitions of terms are based on their common usage prior to 1900. Instructions are given for directions and horary questions. Other topics include Part of Fortune, house systems and much more.

ENCYCLOPEDIA OF ASTROLOGY, Nicholas de Vore. $5.95p ISBN 0-8226-0323-3, 435pp. LIT47. All aspects of astrology are clearly defined in this compendium and may be used by beginning and professional astrologers. Special articles by Charles Jayne and Frederic van Norstrand are also included.

GLOSSARY OF EXPERIENCE ASTROLOGY, Moby Dick. $3.00s 17pp. MOB. More than one hundred fifty thought-provoking and informative definitions and evaluations of astrological terms and concepts are included.

HOW TO USE THE MODERN EPHEMERIDES, Elbert Benjamine. $1.50p ISBN 0-933646-15-1, 64pp. ARI81. The basics of chart calculation are clearly explained using Brotherhood of Light techniques. Computed for midnight and noon, this ephemeris gives the adjusted calculation date, time of exact aspects, eclipses from 1880 to 1980 and the Moon positions favorable to sixty-two activities.

KEYWORDS, Paul R. Grell. $3.00p 31pp. AFA70. Keyword descriptions of the planets, houses and signs are listed here for easy reference.

LAROUSSE ENCYCLOPEDIA OF ASTROLOGY, Jean-Louis Brau, Helen Weaver and Allan Edmands. $17.95c ISBN 0-07-007244-2, 308pp. MCG80. This reference work is intelligible to the general reader. It combines the functions of a dictionary, an encyclopedia and a textbook. Robert Hand says, "This book attempts to go beyond the confines of any one school to enlarge the consciousness of every student of astrology who uses it. It is far better than any existing work of its kind. Every astrologer should have a copy."

NEW DICTIONARY OF ASTROLOGY, Sepharial. $.95p ISBN 0-668-02589-1, ARC.

NEW WAITE'S COMPENDIUM OF NATAL ASTROLOGY, Colin Evans. $7.95c 252pp. WEI71. First published in 1917 this manual gives the basics for chart construction and interpretation. Included are condensed 1880-1980 ephemeris, table of houses, latitude and longitude table and time changes table as well as a review of the meaning of the planets, aspects and houses with character delineation. Instructions with examples are provided.

PRONUNCIATION GUIDE FOR ASTROLOGERS & ASTRONOMERS, T. Patrick Davis. $1.85 16pp. AFA. This is an easy-to-use phonetic guide to the pronunciation of the many cosmic factors.

RAPHAEL'S KEY AND GUIDE TO ASTROLOGY, Raphael. $3.00p ISBN 0-572-00246-7, WFO. This is an introductory astrological guide.

RUNNING PRESS GLOSSARY OF ASTROLOGY TERMS, Leslie Fleming-Mitchell. $2.95p ISBN 0-914294-70-9, 102pp. RUN77. Contains a selection of basic terms and definitions designed to aid the practicing astrologer and to inspire others. The author asserts that once the doors of cosmic-perception and self-perception are opened, the science of astrology will be revealed as one of the connecting links between the human and the divine.

6

Tools and Chart Forms

ASPECT FINDER, Circle Books. $2.25 AFA. This new and improved aspectarian is printed on a heavy card and has a large, aligned inner wheel. It indicates all major and most minor aspects and their orbs.

ASTROCARD, Woodlake Advertising. $1.98 WOO. Twelve cards in a pack. This wallet-size astrological aid has a wheel and a blank table of aspects.

ASTRO-DICE, $9.95 SEK. These twelve-sided dice are intended for use as a horary oracle and come with a set of directions. One each is provided for the planets, signs and houses.

ASTRO-DISC, American Federation of Astrologers. $5.35 AFA. Four in the set: 3" $1.20, 5" $1.70, 4" $1.45, 6" $1.95. These four plastic templates are used for making chart forms.

ASTROLOGICAL GUMMED BOOK PLATES, $1.50 HEA. One for each sign of the zodiac, or twelve of one sign.

ASTROLOGICAL WALL CHART, $1.50 ROS. 16" x 22" heavy paper. Information is provided on the zodiac, planets, their significance and inter-relationships.

ASTROLOGY FLASH CARDS, Astro-Tec. $8.95 ATE. These cards cover dates, planets, rulerships, houses, aspects and so on. They are color-coded by category and an instuction booklet is included.

ASTROLOGY FOR THE MILLIONS BLANKS, Grant Lewi. $3.00 ISBN 0-87542-440-6, LLE. Pad of 100.

ASTROLOGY GAME, Malcolm Dean. $11.95c ISBN 0-8253-0002-9, 256pp. BEA80. This is a guide to understanding the limitations and possibilities of astrology.

CAMBRIDGE CIRCLE HARMONIC CHART FORMS: Nos. 1, 2, 3. $4.50 each, AFA. A pad of 100 forms on quality paper. The form is designed specifically for calculating and presenting harmonic charts and for comparing these with the birth chart or with transits, progressions, etc. Instructions are included. 8 1/2" x 11".

DELUXE COMPLETE ASTROLOGICAL FORMS, A. LeRoi Simmons. $2.25 AQB. 8 1/2" x 11". This large eight inch wheel has a place for transits, progressions, natal planets, aspects and elements. On the reverse side is a complete math form with a step-by-step method for erecting an accurate horoscope, including a detailed example of the math with a complete horoscope. Included is a large logarithm table with instructions. This is a natural zodiac with keywords, symbols and abbreviations. Pads of fifty-five each.

DIAGRAMS FOR PRIMARY ARCS, J. Allen Jones. $4.00p ISBN 0-912368-18-7, GOL70. These diagrams show in detail the necessary arcs and angles with rules and examples for speculum, including Pluto. Also included are examples for directions and other useful information.

DIAGRAMS, $3.00p ROS. 8 1/2" x 11". These astrological and philosophical diagrams and zodiacal drawings are used in Fellowship books.

HEAVEN KNOWS WHAT BLANKS, Grant Lewi. $3.00 ISBN 0-87542-443-0, LLE. Pad of 100.

INSTANTANEOUS ASPECTARIAN, Dorothy Hughes. $2.95 HUG. Finds all aspects to a planet, cusp or placement in the horoscope with one turn of the wheel.

LLEWELLYN NO. 1 HOROSCOPE BLANKS, $3.00 ISBN 0-87542-476-7, LLE. Pad of 100.

LLEWELLYN NO. 4 COMBINATION CHART, $3.00 ISBN 0-87542-479-1, LLE. Pad of 100. Three concentric circles for natal, progressed and transiting planets are divided into twelve segments, with aspect grid.

LLEWELLYN NO. 5 TRANSPARENCY, $3.00 ISBN 0-87542-480-5, LLE. Pad of 50. A semi-transparent combination form can be laid over regular No. 4 for synastry and so on.

LLEWELLYN NO. 9 TYL HOROSCOPE BLANKS, $3.00 ISBN 0-87542-457-0, LLE. Pad of 100. This decorative wheel is divided into twelve houses.

LOGARITHM CARD, American Federation of Astrologers. $.50 AFA.

MEDICINE WHEEL: Earth Astrology, Sun Bean and Wabun. $5.95p ISBN 013-572982-3, 160pp. PRE80. This book combines Indian legend, lore and wisdom in this new system of Earth astrology. It is designed to help guide people not only in their daily living, but on their life path as well.

NATAL HOROSCOPE WORKSHEET, Neil F. Michelsen. $4.00 AST.

PHASE AND ASPECT FINDER, Joanne Wickenburg. $2.50 SEA. Instantly locates Sun/Moon phases and other planetary pairs. At the same time, it reveals the major and minor aspects found within each phase. The movable phase dial has been put on a folder-size back and punched three times for convenient notebook storage.

PRESS TYPE SYMBOLS, American Federation of Astrologers. $4.50 per sheet AFA. Astrological symbols ranging from 1/8″ to 1/2″.

RAPHAEL'S BOOK OF BLANK MAPS, Raphael. $1.50 ISBN 0-572-00253-X, WFO. These twenty-five maps are perforated for easy detachment with instructions for erecting a horoscope. 8 1/2″ by 5 1/2″.

SKY DIAL AND SKY MAP, Magnus Jenson. $4.50; LARGE SKY WALL MAP. $6.50 HEA. The disk turns on a board of ephemeris size. The date and hour circles are in the outer half inch. Inside these follow the zodiac degree circle, and then the decans and the signs in pictures. Essential denotations are made in the center spaces.

STARCARDS: The Astrologer's Handeck, Cosmic Workshop. $12.75 COW. This thirty-six card handeck consists of twelve house cards, sign cards and planet cards. A layout cloth with keywords for the planets, houses and signs and instruction booklet are included.

STAR READING SHEETS, $2.00 HEA.

Want to know when your luck is going to change?

This personal calendar of transits, based on the exact time and place of your birth, forecasts your best days and helps you make the most of them.

In many ways you are a different person every day of your life. You know that from experience. You know that some days are good for getting things done. Other days, every little task is a struggle. Some days you get along with everyone easily and pleasantly, especially the opposite sex. Other days, no one will give you anything you want. Some days are great for bargains. Other days, you shouldn't buy anything.

The Future Wouldn't it be wonderful to be able to look into the future, to know what kinds of days are coming for you and when? In astrology, cycles of psychophysical energy in your life are represented by aspects (angles) from the positions of the planets at a given time in your life to the positions of the planets at the time of your birth. These aspects are called transits. And transits are the most fundamental and reliable tool of astrological forecasting.

Transits Here's an example. At fifty-eight minutes after midnight EST on September 7, 1980, Venus will enter the sign Leo. If you were born with Venus in Leo, then sometime during the following twenty-seven days—the exact time depends on your time of birth—transiting Venus will be conjunct (in the same position as) your natal Venus. This transit marks a favorable time for you to begin a new relationship or renew an old one.

But if Venus is not in Leo in your birth chart, you will not have that transit then. (You'll have others, and you'll have Venus conjunct Venus some other time during the year.) Some transits, like Venus conjunct

Venus, happen once a year or more. Others happen only once in a lifetime. Some transits are fleeting and subtle. Others are long-lasting and profound in their psychological consequences. But whether you know it or not, the moving planets are forming one transit or another to your natal planets *every two or three days!*

Forecasting You owe it to yourself to find out in advance what your transits are going to be. But to find out on your own, you need to consult astronomical tables and find the positions of each of the transiting planets every day and compare them mathematically to the positions of the planets at the time of your birth.

The Astral Guide Luckily, you don't have to do that. Our IBM 370-155 computer is programmed to do the thousands of calculations for you and provide you with a personal calendar of transits based on your exact time and place of birth. This unique calendar will have twelve poster-sized pages, sixteen by twenty-two inches, with your name and birth information printed at the bottom of every page. It will forecast every significant transit to your natal planets that will occur during a twelve month period and explain the meaning of each transit for your life

Astrophoto Your transits for each month of your Astral Guide will be superimposed on an astro-photograph of the Great Nebula in Andromeda against the heavenly blue of deep space. Our new Astral Guide format, created by one of America's leading designers. is so handsome you can hang it in any room in your home.

Cost Before we developed the Astral Guide, only the very rich could afford to have their transits calculated and interpreted daily by professional astrologers. Now you can have the same kind of advice whenever you want it. and it won't cost you thousands or even hundreds of dollars. Many people would consider twenty-four dollars a month a bargain price for a personal transit calendar. But you can have your Astral Guide for much less than twenty-four dollars a month. To find out how and why, read on.

High Speed Printing Your Astral Guide calendar of transits is the result of years of astrological research and computer programming. But since all of that work is now complete you don't have to pay for it. Your Astral Guide will be produced by a computer-driven high-speed printer that prints hundreds of lines per minute. High speed and high volume lower the cost of each Astral Guide tremendously.

Because of this, we are able to offer you your Astral Guide not for twenty-four dollars a month but for twenty-four dollars a year. That's only *$2.00 a month!*

Order Now Your Astral Guide will come to you with an unconditional money-back guarantee. Processing and delivery can take up to three weeks. Fill out the coupon below and send it with $24 today. Your future is waiting for you.

© 1980 Para Research

7

Magazines, Annuals and Calendars

AFA BULLETIN, $15.00 annual subscription AFA.

AMERICAN ASTROLOGY, monthly, $1.00 CLA.

ASPECTS, $5.00 annual subscription AQW.

ASTROLOGICAL REVIEW, $10.00 annual subscription AGA.

ASTROLOGY '81, monthly, $1.50 DEA.

ASTROLOGY FOR THE 80'S, monthly, $.99 CBS.

ASTROLOGY-YOUR DAILY HOROSCOPE, monthly, $.95 CBS.

HOROSCOPE, monthly, $.95 DEL.

HOROSCOPE GUIDE, monthly, $1.25 JBH.

KOSMOS, $15.00 annual subscription ISA.

MACOY ASTROLOGICAL DIGEST, free MAC.

MERCURY HOUR, $15.00 annual subscription MER.

MIDNIGHT HOROSCOPE, monthly, $.95 GLO.

STELLIUM QUARTERLY, $6.00 annual subscription STQ.

TRUE ASTROLOGY FORECAST, quarterly, $1.50 JAL.

ZODIAC, quarterly, $1.50 DEL.

ZOLAR'S LUCKY NUMBER HOROSCOPE, monthly, $1.50 HOR.

Yearbooks

AMERICAN ASTROLOGY DIGEST, $1.50 CLA.

ASTRO-ANALYSIS, $7.95 each GRO.

ASTRO-ANALYSIS 1981 FORECASTS, $6.95 448pp. GRO. Provides daily predictions to help plan personal and business relationships at the most opportune times.

ASTROLOGICAL ALMANAC, $2.00 CBS.

ASTROLOGICAL FORECASTS FOR ALL SIGNS, $6.95 SIM.

ASTROLOGY ANNUAL, $1.95 CBS.

ASTROLOGY ANNUAL REFERENCE BOOK, Marcian MacGregor. $6.95p SYM/ASA.This reference book contains a 1981 ephemeris, a calendar and diary section, and lists the major aspects and Moon phases with sidereal and Greenwich times.

DELL HOROSCOPE YEARBOOK, $1.25 DEL.

GRAPHIC ALMANAC: Your Key to Planning by Natural Cycles, James T. Valliere. $5.95p 40pp. AGR81. The Graphic Almanac traces "the daily cycle of planets rising, passing overhead, setting and passing underfoot" for the entire year.

LLEWELLYN PUBLICATIONS/1981 DAILY PLANETARY GUIDE, $2.95p ISBN 0-87542-472-4, 400pp. LLE80. Designed to assist the reader in planning daily activities, this book contains Moon tables, lunar aspectarian, ephemeris and a pocket calendar. Sections include doing your own personal forecasts and world predictions, a complete guide to gardening and an astrological encyclopedia. Special sections are geared to practical applications of astrology and prediction.

LLEWELLYN PUBLICATIONS/1981 MOON SIGN BOOK, $2.95p ISBN 0-87542-445-7, 500pp. LLE80. The Moon Sign Book contains astrological information which provides a guide for daily activities in accordance with the Moon's cycles. This lunar almanac features month-by-month Sun-sign forecasts, world predictions and the best dates for hunting, fishing, breeding animals and setting eggs.

LOVE SIGNS, $2.95 GRO.

MIDNIGHT HOROSCOPE YEAR BOOK, $1.50 GLO.

MORNINGLAND ASTROLOGICAL DATEBOOK 1981, $5.50 ISBN 0-935146-53-9, MOR. This datebook matches the calendar and features a week-at-a-glance, beautiful mandalas and the planetary positions, including the daily movement of the Moon.

OLD MOORE'S ASTROLOGICAL ALMANAC, $1.25 DEL.

PLANTING BY THE MOON FOR 1981, Simon Best and Nick Kollerstrom. $2.95p ISBN 0-917086-25-2, 128pp. AST81. The expanded United States edition of this grower's guide is written for gardeners and astrologers alike. More than the traditional occult almanac, this easy-to-use book is based on systematic experiments to determine how lunar cycles affect plant metabolism and development. This first edition for 1981 will be followed each year with an up-to-date version.

POCKET ASTROLOGER, Quicksilver Productions, $2.50 ISBN (Eastern Time) 0-930356-26-8; ISBN (Pacific Time) 0-930356-23-3, 64pp. QUI. 4 1/4 x 5 1/2 inches. This color-illustrated pocket-sized version of Celestial Influences includes an ephemeris, calendar and text.

RAPHAEL'S ASTROLOGICAL ALMANAC, Raphael. $1.70p ISBN 0-572-01001-X, WFO. Raphael's almanac contains astrological predictions concerning world events, unique birthday charts, a day-by-day personal forecast for every day of the year, a personal forecast as to the character of babies born on each day of the year, forecasting relating to weather, planting time and more.

SHAMBHALA ASTROLOGICAL COMPANION 1981, Michael Meyer. $2.25p ISBN 0-394-73883-7, 64pp. SHA80. A pocket calendar of astrology designed for easy and frequent reference. 4 1/4" x 6 1/2" with drawings, charts, photos.

YOUR LOVE HOROSCOPE, $1.50 CBS.

YOUR PERSONAL ALMANAC FOR THE ASTROLOGICAL YEAR, $1.95 CBS.

Calendars

ASTROLOGY ANNUAL CALENDAR, Marcian MacGregor. $1.95 SYM/ASA. This calendar shows the weekly planetary position charts and many supplementary tables. The major aspects, new and full Moons, eclipses, solstice dates, solar and lunar ingress and special monthly phenomena are all included.

CELESTIAL GUIDE, Quicksilver Productions. $4.95 ISBN (Eastern Time) 0-930356-25-X; ISBN (Pacific Time) 0-930356-22-5, 160pp. QUI. 4 1/2 x 7 1/2 inches. This weekly astrological engagement calendar includes daily astrological data, an ephemeris, address book and room for notes and appointments.

CELESTIAL INFLUENCES 1981 CALENDAR, James Maynard. $4.95 ISBN (Eastern Time) 0-930356-24-1; ISBN (Pacific Time) 0-939356-21-7, 56pp. QUI. This color-illustrated calendar opens to 11 x 17 inches. The zodiac months within each calendar month, charts of the new Moons and full Moons calculated for Washington, DC and a 1981 ephemeris are included as well as a history on the use of computers in astrology by Douglas Kellogg.

LLEWELLYN PUBLICATIONS/1981 ASTROLOGICAL CALENDAR, $4.95p ISBN 0-87542-446-5, 64pp. LLE80. The fiftieth anniversary edition of this astrological calendar incorporates new design and new art work. The astrological significance of each day of each month is noted. The highs and lows of nature's cycles may be charted with an added feature of the calendar, bio-rhythms for two.

MORNINGLAND ASTROLOGICAL CALENDAR 1981, $4.50 ISBN 0-935146, MOR. Complete with colorful planetary pictures, this reference calendar shows daily planetary movements and provides plenty of space for noting daily events. A key to the planets and the meaning of their movements is provided in the back.

SHAMBHALA ASTROLOGICAL CALENDAR 1981, Michael Meyer. $3.95p ISBN 0-394-73882-9, 48pp. SHA80. This complete and up-to-date astrological calendar is useful and informative for students and professionals alike. 10" x 13" with drawings, charts and photos.

Sun-Sign Books

ASTROSCOPE, $2.95 SIM.

DAY BY DAY HOROSCOPE, $1.75 each TEM.

POCKET GUIDES TO ASTROLOGY, $3.95 each SIM.

SUPER HOROSCOPES 1981, $2.95 each 256pp. GRO.

SYDNEY OMARR'S WEEKLY ASTROLOGICAL GUIDE, $1.25 each SIG.

TOTAL HOROSCOPE, $1.95 ACE.

YOUR PERSONAL FORECAST 1981, $1.95 each 140pp. GRO.

YOUR PERSONAL HOROSCOPE, $1.95 each GRO.

ZODIAC INTERNATIONAL, $1.95 SIM.

Guide to Publishers

ACE Ace Books, Inc., 360 Park Avenue South, New York, NY 10010

ACN Astrology Center of the Northwest, Post Office Box 7127, Station 19, Seattle, WA 98133

AFA American Federation of Astrologers, Inc., Post Office Box 22040, Tempe, AZ 85282

AGA Astrologers Guild of America, Box 75, Old Chelsea Station, New York, NY 10011

AGR Astro-Graphic Services, 217 Rock Harbor Road, Orleans, MA 02653

AMS American School of Astrology, 642 Eagle Rock Avenue, West Orange, NJ 07052

APR/ASA Astro Press, Los Angeles, CA; distributed by Astro-Analytics, 16640 Haynes Street, Van Nuys, CA 91406

AQB Aquarian Book Publishers, 7011 Hammond, Dallas, TX 75223

AQR Aquarian Research Foundation, 5620 Morton Street, Philadelphia, PA 19144

AQU Aquarian Press Ltd., Denington Estate, Wellingborough, Northants NN 8 2RQ England

AQW Aquarius Workshops, Inc., Post Office Box 328, Canoga Park, CA 91303

ARC Arco Publishing, Inc., 219 Park Avenue South, New York, NY 10003

ARE Association for Research and Enlightenment, Inc., Post Office Box 595, Virginia Beach, VA 23451

ARI Aries Press, 5003 West Lawrence Avenue, Chicago, IL 60630

ARN Arcane Publications, York Harbor, ME 03911

ART Arthur Publications, Post Office Box 23101, Jacksonville, FL 32217

ASA Astro-Analytics, 16440 Haynes Street, Van Nuys, CA 91406

ASB Astrological Bureau, 5 Old Quaker Hill Road, Monroe, NY 10950

ASI ASI, 127 Madison Avenue, New York, NY 10016

ASP Astrological and Spiritual Center, 4535 Hohman Avenue, Hammond, IN 46312

AST Astro-Computing Services, Post Office Box 16297, San Diego, CA 92116

ATE Astro-Tec, 16222 Nassau Lane, Huntington Beach, CA 92647

AWH Astrologer on Wheels, Inc., Post Office Box 5255, F.D.R. Station, New York, NY 10150

BAN Bantam Books, Inc., Dept. Fulfillment Services, 2451 South Wolf Road, Des Plaines, IL 60018

BEA Beaufort Books, Inc., 9 East 40th Street, New York, NY 10016

BER Berkley Books, 1050 Wall Street West, Lyndhurst, NJ 07071

BHA Bharat Astrology Institute, New Colony, Srikakulam, Andhra Pradesh, India

CBS CBS Publications, Popular Magazine Group, 1515 Broadway, New York, NY 10036

CHM Church of Mind Awareness, 6641 Gloria Avenue, Van Nuys, CA 91406

CHU Church of Light, Box 76862, Sanford Station, Los Angeles, CA 90076

CLA Clancy Publications, Inc., 2505 North Alvernon Way, Tucson, AZ 85712

CMD C.M.D., Inc., Ruth Armstrong, Box 583, New Monmouth, NJ 07748

COL Colorado Astrological Society, Inc., 1236 Republic Building, Denver, CO 80202

COS Cosmic Cycles, Inc., Post Office Box 2385, Virginia Beach, VA 23452

COW Cosmic Workshop, 1744 Washington Blvd., Venice, CA 90291

CRC CRCS Publications, Post Office Box 20850, Reno, NV 89515

DAR Clara M. Darr Publications, 2527 Broadway, Toledo, OH 43609

DAV Davis Research Reports, Post Office Box 979, Windermere, FL 32786

DEA Ideal Publishing, 2 Park Avenue, New York, NY 10016

DEL Dell Publishing Company, 1 Dag Hammarskjold Plaza, New York, NY 10017

DEN J.M. Dent, 33 Welbeck Street, London W1M 8LX England

DEV DeVorss and Company, Post Office Box 550, Marina Del Rey, CA 90291

DIG Digicomp Research Corporation, Terrace Hill, Ithaca, NY 14850

DOD Carolyn Dodson, 50 Music Square West, United Artist Tower-309, Nashville, TN 37203

DON The Donning Company/Publishers, 5041 Admiral Wright Road, Virginia Beach, VA 23462

DOU Doubleday and Company, Inc., 501 Franklin Avenue, Garden City, NY 11530

DOV Dover Publications, Inc., 180 Varick Street, New York, NY 10014

EDI Editions de L'Apotelesmatique Publications, 130 A Avenue de Broqueville, B-1200 Bruxelles, Belgium

EDO Emma Donath, Post Office Box 563, Dayton, OH 45459

EHU E. & H. Company, Inc., Box 7302, Lewiston, ME 04240

ENT Entwhistle Books, Box 611, Glen Ellen, CA 95442

EPD E.P. Dutton, 2 Park Avenue, New York, NY 10016

EXP Exposition Press, Inc., 50 Jericho Turnpike, Jericho, NY 11753

FLE Fleet Press Corporation, 160 Fifth Avenue, New York, NY 10010

FOW L.N. Fowler Ltd., 1201/3 High Road, Chadwell Heath, Rumford, Essex RM6 4DH England

GLB Golden Light Press, 14 Old Cow Path, Miller Place, NY 11764

GLO Globe Communications Corporation, Post Office Box 674, Rouses Point, NY 12979

GOJ Ivy M. Goldstein-Jacobson, 6374 Encinita Avenue, Temple City, CA 91780

GOL Golden Seal Research, Post Office Box 27821, Hollywood, CA

GRE Bernice Grebner Books, 5137 North Montclair Avenue, Peoria Heights, IL 61614

GRO Grosset & Dunlap, Inc., 51 Madison Avenue, New York, NY 10010

HAM Hamish Hamilton, North Pomfret, VT 05053

HAR Harper & Row, 10 East 53rd Street, New York, NY 10022

HAW Hawkins Enterprising Publications, 416 Keystone Park, Dallas, TX 75243

HBV Hermann Bauer Verlag, Postfach 1 67, Kronenstrabe 2-4, 7800 Freiburg, Germany

HEA Health Research, Post Office Box 70, Mokelumne Hill, CA 95245

HIC Isabel M. Hickey, 35 Maple Street, Watertown, MA 02172

HIE Hieratic Publishing Company, Post Office Box 133, Medford, MA 02155

HOR Horoscope Properties, Inc., 300 West 43rd Street, New York, NY 10036

HOU House of Astrology, 1449 Messenger Court, South Euclid, OH 44121

HUG Dorothy B. Hughes, 2322 6th Avenue, Seattle, WA 98121

HUN Hunter House Inc., Publishers, 748 East Bonita Avenue, Suite 105, Pomona, CA 91765

INT Inner Traditions/Destiny Books, 377 Park Avenue South, New York, NY 10016

ISA International Society for Astrological Research, 70 Melrose Place, Montclair, NJ 07042

JAK Jakubowsky, 1565 Madison Street, Oakland, CA 94612

JAL Jalart House, Inc., Post Office Box 642, Scottsdale, Az 85252

JBH JBH Publishing, 350 Madison Avenue, Cresskill, NJ 07626

JOV Jove Publications, Inc., 200 Madison Avenue, New York, NY 10016

KAM K.H. Ambjornson, 433 Melrose Avenue, San Francisco, CA 94127

LAB Laboratorie d'Etude des Relations entre Rythmes Cosmiques et Psychophysiologiques, 3 Rue Amyot, 77005 Paris, France

LAG Lambert-Gann Publishing Company, Box O, Pomeroy, WA 99347

LIT Littlefield, Adams & Company, 81 Adams Drive, Totowa, NJ 07512

LLE Llewellyn Publications, 213 East 4th Street, St. Paul, MN 55101

LUC Lucis Publishing Company, 866 United Nations Plaza, Suite 566-567, New York, NY 10017

MAC Macoy Publishing & Masonic Supply Company, Inc., Post Office Box 9759, Richmond, VA 23228

MAM MacMilliam Company, 866 3rd Avenue, New York, NY 10022

MAS Sophie Mason and Mary Lou Shepherd, 7780 Jill Drive, Parma, OH 44134

MCG McGraw-Hill Book Company, 1221 Avenue of the Americas, New York, NY 10020

MER Mercury Hour, Edith Custer, C-7 3509 Waterlick Road, Lynchburg, VA 24502

MOB Moby Dick, 1136 Union Mall, Suite 706, Honolulu, HI 96813

MOH Mohan Enterprises, Post Office Box 8334, Rochester, NY 14618

MOR Morningland Publications, Inc., 2634 East 7th Street, Long Beach, CA 90804

MOT Motivation Development Centre, Post Office Box 25643, Albuquerque, NM 87125

NES NESA, Frances Sakoian, One Monadnock Road, Arlington, MA 02174

NEW New Age Library, Post Office Box 120, Bergenfield, NJ 07621

NIN Ninth Sign Publications, Post Office Box M525, Hoboken, NJ 07030

NOY Noyes Press, Mill Road at Grand Avenue, Park Ridge, NJ 07656

NPC New Castle Publishing Company, Inc., Post Office Box 7589, Van Nuys, CA 91409

OMA Omega Associates, Post Office Box 801, Midlothian, IL 60445

PAR Para Research, Dept. IP, Whistlestop Mall, Rockport, MA 01966

PEN Penguin Books, 625 Madison Avenue, New York, NY 10022

PHP Patronage House Publishers, Post Office Box 53, Boston, MA 02113

PHR Philosophical Research Society, 3910 Los Feliz Blvd., Los Angeles, CA 90027

PIN Pinnacle Books, 271 Madison Avenue, New York, NY 10016

PRA Practical Astrology, Box 163, South Weymouth, MA 02190

PRE Prentice-Hall, Box 500, Englewood Cliffs, NJ 07632

QUI Quicksilver Productions, Post Office Box 340, Ashland, OR 97520

RAN Random House Inc., 201 East 50th Street, New York, NY 10022

REC Recent Advances, 64 Coghlan Road, Subiaco 6008, Western Australia

ROS Rosicrucian Fellowship, 222 Mission Avenue, Oceanside, CA 92054

ROU Routledge & Kegan Paul, 9 Park Street, Boston, MA 02108

RUN Running Press, 38 South 19th Street, Philadelphia, PA 19103

SAB Sabian Publishing Society, 2324 Norman Road, Stanwood, WA 98292

SAG Sagittarius Rising, P.O. Box 252, Arlington, MA 01760

SEA Search, Post Office Box 162, Northgate Station, Seattle, WA 98125

SEE Seed Center, Box 658, Garberville, CA 95440

SEK Seek-It Publications, Post Office Box 1074, Birmingham, MI 48012

SHA Shambhala Publications, Inc., 1123 Spruce Street, Boulder, CO 80302

SIG Signet, 1633 Broadway, New York, NY 10019

SIM Simon & Schuster, 1230 Avenue of the Americas, New York, NY 10020

STA Star Astrology, 449 McCarty, San Antonio, TX 78216

STE Stein & Day Publishers, Scarborough House, Briarcliff Manor, NY 10510

STQ Stellium Quarterly, Post Office Box 12973, El Paso, TX 77912

STY Stymie Publications, Anaheim, CA; distributed by Astro-Analytics, 16440 Haynes Street, Van Nuys, CA 91406

SUE Sue Ann, Box 2, Northhaven, CT 06473

SYM Symbols & Signs, North Hollywood, CA; distributed by Astro-Analytics, 16440 Haynes Street, Van Nuys, CA 91406

TAI TAI Books, Box 927, McLean, VA 22101

TAY Maxine Taylor, Post Office Box 52861, Atlanta, GA 30355

TEM Tempo Books, 360 Park Avenue, New York, NY 10010

THA Thames and Hudson Ltd., 30-34 Bloomsbury Street, London WC1B 3QP England

THE Theosophical Publishing House, 306 West Geneva Road, Wheaton, IL 60187

THS Theosophical Society Book Department, 119 Northeast 62nd Street, Miami, FL 33138

TIA TIA Publications, Post Office Box 45558, Los Angeles, CA 90045

UNI Union Press, 3109 Deakin Street, Berkeley, CA 94705

URA Uranus Publishing Company, 5050 Calatrana Drive, Woodland Hills, CA 91364

VAN Vantage Press, Inc., 516 West 34th Street, New York, NY 10001

VUL Vulcan Books, Inc., Post Office Box 25616, Seattle, WA 98125

WEI Samuel Weiser, Inc., Post Office Box 612, York Beach, Maine 03910

WFO W. Foulsham & Company, Ltd., Yeovil Road, Slough SL1 4JH, England

WHA Whatever Publishing, 158 E. Blithedale, Mill Valley, CA 94941

WHE The White Eagle Publishing Trust, New Lands, Liss, Hampshire GU33 7HY England

WIL Wilshire Book Company, 12015 Sherman Road, North Hollywood, CA 91605

WIM William Morrow & Company, Inc., 105 Madison Avenue, New York, NY 10016

WOO Woodlake Advertising, 15 Clubhouse Drive, Woodbury, CT

Now there's a horoscope for the two of you

It takes more than love to make a relationship work. It takes understanding. And understanding comes from knowing. Do you really *know* the one you love?

By combining new astrology techniques with humanistic psychology, scientific analysis, and computer accuracy, Para Research has developed a new way of looking at a relationship.

Now there is a horoscope for the two of you. It's the Astral Composite, the world's first computerized *composite* horoscope. This 10,000-word report takes a look at your relationship by actually casting a horoscope of the relationship itself.

Until now astrologers have compared two people's horoscopes by superimposing one on the other. Such a comparison views the people as individuals who happen to be involved in a relationship. This is helpful to a point, but misleading and incomplete.

The Astral Composite is different from comparison horoscopes. As its name implies, it is a *composite* of the two natal charts. With this method a third chart is created, a chart of the relationship itself. When two people come together to form a relationship, something new emerges. They are still the same two people, of course, but together they are something else as well. Together they are the relationship. This is what the Astral Composite is all about.

This method of analyzing human relationships was developed about 30 years ago. Today most astrologers still adhere to the old comparison method. One astrologer, Robert Hand, has further developed the composite technique for a new kind of horoscope. The result of his work is the first complete text on composite horoscopes in any language. It is now available to you as the Astral Composite from

Para Research, America's leading producer of computer horoscopes.

What does the Astral Composite consist of? An Astral Composite is three charts in one. First the computer calculates the natal charts of the two people involved. Next these two charts are combined to form a third chart, the chart of the relationship. One plus one equals three. This is followed by a reading of the chart, describing the potentialities of the relationship. All the factors of love, money, and friendship are taken into account. This helps point out the kind of relationship that works best for the two of you. You may be great together as lovers, but when it comes to a more lasting commitment you may be heading for trouble. Better to be prepared than to fall into a situation unknowingly.

The Astral Composite not only points out the strengths and weaknesses in your relationship, it also offers astrological advice on how to improve the relationship. Even the most difficult planetary combinations in the composite chart can be turned into positive forces. With your Astral Composite you will be able to enrich your relationship to the fullest degree.

Specifically, this is what you get when you order your Astral Com-

posite at the remarkable introductory price of only $19.

• Three charts: a natal chart of each person plus the composite.

• An introduction describing the meaning of each planet.

• Planets in the houses: divisions of the horoscope describing different areas of the relationship. The positions of the Sun and Moon show the main emphasis of the relationship.

• All major planetary aspects: these are important to understanding the dynamics of the relationship. Conjunctions, sextiles, squares, trines and oppositions are included as well as aspects to the Ascendant.

• Accurate calculations: an IBM computer is used to provide accuracy to the nearest minute of arc. (Our accuracy depends on accurate birth data. See coupon below.)

• Text by Robert Hand: Mr. Hand is a specialist in the field of astrology for relationships. He is the first and only astrologer to write an extensive work on composite charts.

• Approximately 10,000 words and 25 pages in easy-to-read, beautifully bound book format.

• Money-back guarantee: the Astral Composite is unconditionally guaranteed by Para Research. If unsatisfied, simply return the horoscope for a full refund.

We would like to emphasize that this is a full-dimensional analysis of a relationship. There is no other horoscope in the world that can compare to the Astral Composite. It represent the most exciting development in astrology since the invention of the computer. It is truly unique.

You are invited to partake in what we feel will be a revealing experience for the two of you...and your relationship.

© *1980 Para Research*

Author Index